LEAVE YOUR TEARS IN MOSCOW

Leave Your Tears in Moscow

by BARBARA ARMONAS

as told to A. L. NASVYTIS

J. B. LIPPINCOTT COMPANY

PHILADELPHIA AND NEW YORK

To those Americans who helped my husband and
daughter so much in their twenty-year fight to
reunite our family

A. L. Nasvytis wishes to express his thanks to Mrs. Barbara Snelbaker for her very able technical assistance in preparing the manuscript.

Contents

1

Good-bye to John

"DON'T WORRY, BARBARA," said my husband, kissing me good-bye as he left for America. "I'm sure that in a few months you can join me and be safely out of this mess."

Neither he nor I had any foreboding that this kiss would be the last for almost twenty years of terrible suffering for my son and me. My family has been united again due to the endless struggle of my husband and our daughter, Donna. Even today, I can hardly believe that our ordeals are over and that the rest of our lives can be spent safely and peacefully—no one will order me to smile, to work, to go to meetings and, most of all, no one will suddenly arrest me for no reason.

I was born on a small farm in northern Lithuania and spent my youth there in my parents' home. I met my husband, John Armonas, in 1929 and we were married the same year. John was born in the United States of Lithuanian immigrant parents and had spent his youth in Cleveland. Curious to see the land of his ancestry, he had come to Lithuania as a tourist, yet he not only married there but bought an eighty-seven-acre farm in the village of Suostas, thirty miles from my birthplace. Indeed, this was not a bad deal. He could rent the farm for more than American banks at that time were paying in interest for equal money invested.

After our marriage, John returned to Cleveland and, a few months later, the usual procedures of immigration completed, I followed him. We lived on East Forty-seventh Street, near Superior. John worked in a dairy and I worked in tailor shops for a few years. We lived peacefully and happily and even managed to save money.

In 1934 our daughter was born and in 1935 we decided to visit Lithuania. I was especially anxious to see my parents and relatives and the trip was within the reach of our financial resources.

We were surprised at the changes in Lithuania. The country was prospering, cities were growing, and modern schools and highways had been built. I hardly recognized our county town of Birzai. By changing from grain to more profitable dairy, poultry, and cattle farming, and by improving their agricultural methods, the farmers had increased their income and pulled the entire Lithuanian economy together.

We liked the country very much, especially my husband's farm. While we were there the man who rented it canceled his lease, so we decided to stay on and manage the farm ourselves.

In that quiet, friendly countryside we did not pay too much attention when, after a few years, political clouds began to grow dark and dangerous. The aggressive behavior of Hitler's Germany and the growing tension with Poland, both countries bordering ours to the south and west, bothered us somewhat. During this time Germany annexed the Lithuanian Baltic city of Klaipeda, on the grounds that this Lithuanian province had been a part of the German Imperium before the First World War.

John decided then that we should move back to the United States. He went alone first to look around but when he reached America he became more alarmed, for everyone there believed that war was imminent. He decided to return to Lithuania immediately, sell the property, and move his family permanently to the United States. He arrived in July, 1939, and we began preparations to leave. Seven weeks later war broke out, making travel to the United States for ordinary citizens almost impossible.

There remained nothing to do but wait.

Lithuania declared complete neutrality but the situation was precarious since the Polish-German war theater was directly on our border. After Russia attacked Poland from behind and conquered the eastern provinces, Lithuania acquired a very long border with the U.S.S.R. Thousands of Polish officers crossed over and were interned in our country.

The tension and dark premonitions increased when Russia demanded, by threat of force, to be allowed to establish military bases in Lithuania and her neighboring states of Latvia and Estonia, supposedly to help us maintain our neutrality. Confronted with such a force and having no support from other world powers, the Baltic countries could only agree. Various friendship, respected sovereignty and mutual aid treaties were signed with Russia. No one knew at this time that the fate of our country had already been decided when Hitler and Stalin had signed a secret treaty leaving the Baltic states entirely in the sphere of Russian influence.

Suddenly, eight months after these military bases were established, Russian armies invaded the Baltic states both from across the border and from these bases. This was done at a time when all world attention was focused on the German attack on France and the evacuation at Dunkirk. In spite of repeated declarations from Russia that Lithuanian internal politics were to be unaffected by the march of Russian troops, a new government friendly to the Communists was forced upon us.

The Lithuanian president managed to escape. The heads of the Latvian and Estonian governments remained and were forced to put their signatures to various acts. When they were no longer useful, they disappeared. Most of the Lithuanian politicians believed the Russian promises and remained in the country although during the first days of the occupation they could have escaped to Germany.

One of the first acts was to replace all Lithuanian border police with Russian guards and to seal off the border with the West. After this the terror grew. Everyone understood that Lithuania had lost its independence and sooner or later would be incorporated into Russia. The mood of the Lithuanian population, except for a few Communists, was beyond description.

Living in a remote province in a farming area, we didn't feel the pressures as quickly as the people in the intellectual and political centers, but many terrifying rumors reached us. It was told that many influential persons had been arrested in Vilnius, Kaunas and other cities. After the occupation was complete, a broad amnesty was declared. Communist activity in Lithuania had been illegal but in addition to Communists many persons were released who were in prison due to criminal behavior.

As the activity of the Communist organization increased, we began to feel the system more severely. The police were replaced with Soviet militia made up mostly of Communists and their followers. They had certain difficulties in establishing their organization in our township. It appeared at first that out of a population of eleven thousand we had only two secret members of the Communist Party, but the number of fellow travelers grew rapidly, recruited mainly from the so-called victims of the nationalist government.

New elections were ordered. Before the elections in our remote community, however, important citizens such as the veterinarian, mayor, and chief of security police, Mr. Vaisnoras, were arrested. Mr. Vaisnoras is still in prison in Moscow after twenty years. On the single slate of candidates, all the names were absolutely unknown to any of us. The newly established People's Militia forced the people to vote by going from house to house with threats of reprisals if they did not do so.

Like everyone else, we were frightened and saddened by seeing the freedom of our little country crushed. Relief came when my husband received a letter from the American Legation saying that preparations had been completed to evacuate American citizens from Lithuania. The letter also stated that only John, Donna, and John, Jr., then eight months old, could leave as American nationals. I, having no claim to American citizenship except through marriage, would not be considered eligible and could not leave with them. My husband hurried to Kaunas where the American Legation was located. The American Consul, though he could not arrange for my immediate departure, said he felt it could easily be managed in the near future. He advised John to leave our son with me, which he thought would be helpful in getting us out later.

I was uneasy about remaining alone with my baby son but confident that I could join my husband very soon. Who would be interested, I thought, in a quiet, ordinary family like ours? We said good-bye on our farm. The cries of our daughter as she demanded that I go with them remained vividly in my memory for all my twenty years of separation from her.

John and Donna left Lithuania August 8, 1940, going through Berlin, Stockholm and Petsamo, Finland, then leaving on an American ship for New York. Shortly afterwards I received a letter from John saying that he had made all the arrangements at the State Department in Washington and was already in Cleveland working at the U. S. Steel Spring Company. I also received a letter from the American Consul saying that in two months another transport would be arriving and all remnants of American families could leave the country then.

The American Consul made certain that my documents were in order and then advised me to go to the Internal Ministry in Kaunas to apply for an exit visa. I went there many times and the officials always permitted me to fill out questionnaires and sign various papers, promising each time to get me the exit permit. Once a newly appointed Russian official, elderly and with a sad face, surprised me. He looked around and, seeing no one within listening distance, whispered, "Do not waste your effort—you will never obtain the permit."

In the meantime the communization of Lithuania was progressing rapidly. The recently elected Parliament decided to ask Russia to incorporate Lithuania into the U.S.S.R. A delegation was sent to Moscow, and Stalin and the Soviet House of Representatives "reluctantly" agreed to accept. This happened on August 3, 1940. Later we found that not only was the so-called Parliament elected from members of the Communist Party, but all the speeches made and decisions reached by this Parliament had been prepared by a planning committee in Moscow before the occupation.

Now all foreign diplomats left the country. Systematically, all Lithuanian institutions were replaced by Russian ones. Russian currency was introduced on a one-to-one basis but prices for everyday necessities increased tenfold. All large enterprises such as banks and factories were nationalized. Many responsible people, the leaders of these institutions, were replaced and some of them were jailed.

The entire nation was in a state of shock. Lithuania had lost her national freedom and after twenty-one years of independence again experienced Russian occupation, this time of a different type. Now everything was wrapped in a lie. The newspapers from the big cities kept their old names, but sneered at everything that had been a part of Lithuania before the occupation, while praising the new persecutions and terrors as liberation, freedom, and the opportunity for improvement of our standard of living.

The Lithuanian flag and national insignia were prohibited. Singing of the Lithuanian anthem was forbidden too and considered a treasonable act.

Many meetings were organized. Propagandists came from the big cities to laud the new freedoms and always ended by proposing to send a telegram to Mr. Stalin in the Kremlin thanking him for the liberation of our beloved country. Everyone was afraid to resist such proposals and usually they were accepted unanimously.

The teachers were especially unhappy. In a short time all the schoolbooks were changed. Everything that had been good now was called bad and the teachers were forced to tell lies to their students. There was no way to resist. Reluctance led to dismissal or, even worse, being jailed.

The people were horrified by the manner in which the Communist police arrested their victims. Generally, arrests were made outside of the home; men, and women, simply didn't return. No one knew what had happened to them, or where they were, and it could only be guessed that they had been arrested.

The economy grew worse day by day. Prices soared and many items of necessity disappeared completely from the shop windows. Small businesses and stores were nationalized, as were apartment houses. The residents of small houses had the right to a certain square footage of living space per person. Those who had more were forced to accept roomers, even whole families, sent to them by the newly established housing offices.

After the border with Russia was opened, thousands of Russian citizens swarmed into Lithuania and started buying everything available. We were very surprised by this because Lithuanian tourists and newsmen who visited Russia kept telling us about the country's vast progress and impressive achievements.

The workers on my farm very often had to attend meetings, where they were incited against the landowners and told that they were being exploited and that after private ownership was destroyed their living conditions would improve immensely. Still, private property and farming were permitted. Only acreage in excess of seventy-three acres was nationalized so I lost fourteen acres and had an administrator appointed from the government to control my farming. I was now having trouble with my workers so one of my brothers came to live with me and help to run the farm.

During this time my husband was doing everything he could to get us out. In the winter I visited Kaunas again and was told that the first step towards obtaining an exit visa was to pay the fare in dollars from Kaunas through all of Russia to Vladivostok to the Russian Intourist. I wrote this to my husband and he sent two hundred dollars for the trip. After this, when my departure was delayed, the Russian Embassy in Washington refused even to answer his letters of inquiry.

The winter passed somehow. We had enough food and wood and farmers were not bothered too much. But in the villages and markets the people were afraid to talk about politics or discuss the steadily worsening living conditions. Political arrests were still going on and rumors were spread that many Lithuanians were being forced to act as spies among their friends, reporting everyone who made unfriendly remarks about Communism.

Once I met a good friend and started to complain about my detention until he warned me:

"Don't talk this way to me, Barbara, especially if anyone else is listening. I have agreed to work with the secret police and must report everything to them. It was the only way to save myself from arrest."

In the spring of 1941 each farmer was ordered to deliver a certain amount of grain to the state immediately. The amount was excessive and impossible to meet. I still had not given up hope of getting out and thought by fulfilling this demand I might better my chances so I sold half of my cattle and met the quota. Later many of those who failed to deliver the entire amount were put in concentration camps. Some larger owners in the neighborhood lost their farms completely. They were evicted and so-called "sow-hoz," state-owned farms, emerged.

People working on the state-owned farms were very much surprised; now they were paid much less than under the capitalist system.

On June 14, 1941, an event happened which I will never forget. A few days before, we had noticed increased truck and military movement on the roads. During the night of June 13-14, without any warning, many families were awakened and told that they were being deported and had thirty minutes to collect their belongings. Some of the victims were acquaintances of mine—mayor, Mr. Dinsmonas, and his family, some teachers in our public schools, and our very good friends, the village policeman, Mr. K. Pavilonis, his wife and two daughters, eight years old and five months old. Mrs. Pavilonis was our son's godmother. They were all crowded into cattle cars which stood in the railroad yards for several days. I tried to reach the cars at the station nearest our town where the Pavilonis family was kept, but the station was so closely guarded by soldiers that I couldn't get close. Somehow I did manage to find the car in which they were, and was able to give them two hundred rubles by bribing a soldier to hand it to them. No one knew how these people were selected or why, or where they would be sent, and no one knew of any law in Russia which entitled the government to such an action. It is thought that about forty thousand Lithuanians were deported. They were not the last.

After this deportation we all lived in terror. No one knew when another such blow would fall, or who the next victims would be. Every day life became more dangerous and unpredictable. Rumors ran wild about coming persecutions of farmers and that they would be forced to join collective farms. Ten months had passed since my husband had left and no progress had been made toward our reunion. I didn't dare think about the possibility that I might have to stay here with my son for a long time.

2

The Germans Come

ON JUNE 21, 1941, the Germans attacked Russia. Since Lithuania is on the German border it was invaded first. In our remote province we got news of the invasion only after noon when German airplanes were seen flying over. All week long we had seen Russian vehicles retreating along the roads and after seven days, without fighting, German vehicles appeared. No one was afraid of the war; instead, there was rejoicing that the Communists and their system were being chased out. At first our joy was intense. Our farmers went to the highway, taking the Germans milk, juices and other gifts. The soldiers seemed friendly and harmless.

The wave of indignation against the Communist regime got out of hand when freed Lithuanian leaders reported that many political prisoners had been murdered in their cells by Russian guards. Other prisoners were marched towards Russia and when the Russians felt that they could not move fast enough to avoid the Germans, they were massacred east of Lithuania in the Belorussian forests. It is said that seven to eight thousand Lithuanian prisoners perished on this march. The rage of the population was so

intense that some captured Communists were lynched before the Germans could save them.

Very soon, however, there was disappointment that the
invading German armies did not recognize Lithuania as
politically independent but treated us as a conquered country which must deliver goods, especially farm products, to
the Germans. Even so, they didn't seriously interfere with
the social structure or living habits of the people. The
schools began operating again, using the old programs of
national Lithuania. The Lithuanian national anthems and
flag were permitted. There were, however, many restrictions, especially in political life, while organizations were
regulated and newspapers were heavily censored.

Next, the German administration started to persecute the
Jewish minority. In northern Lithuania there were only a
few Jewish people, mostly small shopkeepers, tailors, and
craftsmen. A few days after the occupation, the Gestapo,
arriving just behind the troops, arrested them all from the
small towns in our county and herded them into a barbed-
wire-enclosed section of Pasvalys which the Germans called
a "ghetto." Many attempts were made to get food to the
prisoners but the area was heavily guarded and everyone
who tried was turned back and closely questioned. Obviously it was dangerous to have any contact with these un-
fortunate people.

About two months after the establishment of the ghetto,
the German police ordered all the farmers in the neighborhood to start digging big ditches about two miles from
Pasvalys and one mile from my native village. There was
no reason given but, as usual, the air was thick with rumors.
Some said the Russians were coming back and this was to

be a part of the German field defenses. Another story was that these were for the graves for the coming massacre of the Jews, but we couldn't believe that; it was too fantastic even for those perilous times.

One morning about ten o'clock I was visiting relatives in Pasvalys when a neighbor hurried into the house looking very pale. He said the Germans were driving the Jewish people from Pasvalys towards the ditches. While we were talking we heard gunfire and understood what was happening. I hid my face in pillows but there was no escape from the horrible picture of the murder of these poor helpless people.

This was a terrible blow to the neighborhood. The story was whispered from person to person. Everyone was surprised that the Jews showed no resistance, and that a few Lithuanians took part in this terrible deed, men who belonged to the police force guided by the German police which had charge of the massacre in our area. One farmer remarked, "It is enough to establish a hell; the devils will come."

Now the future seemed hopeless. If the Germans won there was no hope of having a decent life, but if the Germans lost the Russians would return and they were even worse. The only faint hope we could see was that if the democracies won, they would surely provide the right of self-determination for us and then we would again be an independent nation. We all listened to the Allied radio although it was strictly prohibited. Mostly we listened to the BBC to find out how the war was going. It was our only way of getting any real news and we felt it was worth the risk.

My life was now a day-to-day struggle for survival. Because I had already sold my farm equipment and animals, I couldn't farm so I bartered all my land to my neighbors for a small amount of grain and other farm products.

Life was dull and held no great hope for the future, but we were still alive. I was getting letters regularly from my husband through the Red Cross and I even managed to tell him about the deportation of Johnny's godmother. I made no attempt to leave the country for there was no way to travel and when war broke out between Germany and the United States, I was afraid of possible persecution because of John's citizenship, but I wasn't bothered at all.

The Germans were very arrogant while the war was going well for them. The administration in the Baltic states treated us as second-rate people, with a special system of rationing, and in the larger cities there were certain shops where the Germans, not only military personnel but civilians as well, could get goods which were denied the local population. The food and grain quotas set by the Germans were large but not impossible to meet. It was very hard to get goods in the stores but the black market was thriving. The economic rate of exchange was similar to that of the Russians; a pair of shoes, for instance, cost more than the whole monthly pay of a city worker.

When the course of the war turned against the Germans, they changed their tactics. They encouraged Lithuanians to join the work battalions supporting German troops at the front, but most men refused to help them, much as they hated the Russians, because they had learned to hate the Germans too. Only a few youths answered the call and in reprisal the Germans partially closed the universities and sent some prominent Lithuanians to their concentration camps.

The local municipalities were then ordered to recruit a certain number of workers to be sent to Germany. Everyone tried to escape this too. The morale of the country deteriorated every day. Factory workers, clerks in warehouses and distribution offices stole whatever they could, claiming that they were not stealing from the owners but from the occupants, an attitude that was practically unknown in my country before 1939.

In the first days of the war the Germans had captured millions of Russian soldiers. At first they were treated badly. They died by the thousands and yet they were mostly anti-Communists who had surrendered because they had no interest in fighting for the Soviet. Now, when the Red Army was pushing Germany back, the Germans tried to organize defensive armies from the remnants of these prisoners but it was too late. If they had been allowed to fight when first captured instead of being so badly mistreated, they would have made good defenders. Now both their morale and numbers were low.

More and more people began talking about the approach of the Red Army. The BBC kept us informed of the situation on the German east front. Now that the Russians were approaching again, we had to decide quickly what was best for us to do. Some people abandoned everything and fled towards Germany; most of them had been persecuted by the Russians or had relatives already imprisoned by them.

I didn't know what to do. It was very hard for me to get away since Johnny was only five and I had no one to help me. I was not a political person and wasn't very much afraid of persecution by the Russians. Now that America and Russia were allies I thought I might find it easier to leave for the United States than it had been before. Then, too, if I went to Germany I knew that I would be exposing both of us to Allied bombings.

After much thought I decided to stay where I was.

3

The Red Army Returns

As PROTECTION from possible shelling, my farm help and I dug a ditch in our garden about fifty yards from the house. We also buried some food and our more valuable belongings. It was fortunate that we were prepared because this time the war was very different from the Russian retreat. The Germans put up tremendous resistance in our area and we lived on the front for about six weeks.

On July 26, 1944, the Russians broke through for the first time but were repulsed the next day by the Germans. Sometimes the front changed hands three times in a single day. We enlarged our ditch in the garden and soon the families of five neighbors were staying with us. Sometimes we dared not raise our heads above the level of the ditch for thirty-six hours at a time. In the quieter intervals we came out to look for food.

Amazingly, despite the battle that raged around us, our house was unburned and almost undamaged. All the farm-houses near the highway were shelled and burned but ours was a little more remote. As a precaution I had taken all my furniture and clothes outdoors and because there was no rainfall during these long weeks they came through very well too.

Neither side bothered with us. After the front had passed, guards with rifles searched our ditch, counted the people and left us unharmed. Once the Germans counterattacked, took a few Russian prisoners and immediately shot them. Later when they had moved on and it was a little quieter we came out of our ditch and saw a young Russian soldier hiding in our cabbage garden. He was a Mongol about seventeen years old. He jumped up, came towards us and started to cry in broken Russian, "Don't shoot me, I have a mother and she loves me."

We didn't know what to do with him. If we kept him with us and the Germans found him they would kill him and punish us. To turn him in to the Germans seemed inhuman; neither the Germans nor the Russians were taking any prisoners. Finally, one of our women suggested that since he was young and small we dress him as a girl, give him a pail and send him to the cow pasture which was in the direction of the Russian Army. We never knew what happened to him.

It was remarkable that in spite of the severe fighting and bombings, very few local people were lost. We were horrified to see the lack of concern for human life displayed by the Russian Army. As they retreated the Germans laid mine fields here and there. When the Russians came they ordered their soldiers to march through these fields with complete disregard for the casualties. In general, Russian casualties always ran higher than German even during the German retreat.

Finally, after a long seesaw battle, the Russians took over

again in our section. My house was used for field staff quarters. I had no complaint, for the soldiers and officers behaved well. I even managed to send a letter to John telling him that we were still alive. My son played with the officers and when he saw an airplane always told everyone, "Here comes my father." One young officer, probably a Georgian, became friendly and I told him my story. He was going on leave to the Caucasus through Moscow, and agreed to mail a letter for me. He said we were friends now with America but nevertheless asked me to translate the letter, written in Lithuanian, into Russian for him and warned me to write nothing more than I told him.

Immediately after the army moved in, secret police detachments came, just as the Gestapo had followed the German armies. They started investigating and taking complaints. In the old Bolshevist fashion people started to disappear but this time it was not only the men but whole families that were missing. It seemed that they were being silently and secretly deported. There were rumors that they were being killed but there was no proof. We lived under the fear of new deportations, the memory of the Jewish massacre, and wild tales about the behavior of the Russian Army. Everyone was talking about the extermination of the entire Tartar Crimean nation. Rumor had it that the Russians had sealed off the east Prussian border to prevent food from getting in and that the people were in danger of starving unless they could escape to eastern Germany. South Lithuania was overflowing with hungry exhausted German refugees. A few even reached our county and we helped them as much as we could. We all wondered if a similar fate was planned for Lithuania.

We began to receive letters from Siberia, from the relatives and friends deported back in 1941 and were shocked to learn that only a small fraction had survived the hard living conditions there.

In the meantime Russia had issued an edict that all men from the age of seventeen to advanced years (I don't remember the exact figure) were to be recruited into the army. Having seen the Russian methods of fighting, people felt that to be a fresh recruit, and not of Russian nationality, would be almost sure death.

Finally, many youths decided that it would be better to die in a resistance movement than to be helplessly slaughtered. Surely, a few months spent in a resistance movement against the Communist occupation could only help the cause for Lithuanian independence. It wouldn't be too dangerous for the freedom fighters themselves because the end of the war was imminent and independence was sure to follow. Everyone believed in the Atlantic Charter and that in the new order after World War II, each nation would have the right of self-determination.

The Russians took immediate action against the freedom fighters. In the winter of 1945 they searched each village for men of military age and when they found such men at home without proof of release from the army, automatically sentenced them to ten years or more in a concentration camp.

The freedom fighters had no trouble collecting weapons and ammunition from the battlefields and they showed remarkable resistance to the Russians. For more than two years most Lithuanian villages and farm areas were ruled by the Russians by day and the freedom fighters at night.

Every day the Russian attempts at suppression became more cruel. There were many stories about battles and punishments in other areas. In our vicinity there were not enough forested areas for them to hide in but even so we had sharp conflicts which caused tremendous suffering.

This freedom movement which started in 1945 persisted until 1953, over eight years. Some brave men survived in the forests for the entire time, although their cause was doomed; without supplies, four hundred miles inside the Soviet Imperium, they had no way to continue the struggle.

Some young sons of my friends who had gone to the forests would come to my house at night, asking what I heard from my husband in America. They knew the situation was hopeless and still they dreamed of America. I remember one night I told these boys, "I have pity for you. Perhaps there is some way to avoid this fighting." They answered, "We know that we will die, but at least we will have proven to the world that Lithuanians are not selling their freedom cheap." Yet apparently no one in the free world knew about the freedom fighters in Lithuania, so even this hope was in vain.

Everyone in the free world knew about the Czech village of Lidice which was burned and all the men there killed because the local Czech partisans had shot a high German officer, but no one heard about the many Lithuanian villages which were burned and all their inhabitants machine-gunned regardless of age or sex.

Not being successful in eliminating the partisans, the Communist police started a tremendous reprisal action against their relatives. If a partisan was captured and identified, the next of kin were arrested and sent to prison and all known relatives were deported to Siberia. The partisans later always carried emergency hand grenades so that when they were surrounded or captured they could blow off their heads and not endanger their families.

In 1946 in the village of Tilinava, about five miles from my house, the Communists were told of a barn near the forest where some partisans were sleeping. The police quietly prepared for action. They sent soldiers and for eight miles around blocked off all the roads with machine gun emplacements. Then they attacked. The barn was fired with flame throwers and grenades and machine guns were used on the sleeping men. Twenty-four bodies were found in the vicinity. How many had been inside the barn no one knows. These twenty-four bodies were taken to the market place of our county and kept there for over a week during the hot summer days, while the secret police watched from a hide-out. Anyone passing by who showed a sign of emotion was arrested and all his relatives were deported to Siberia.

During the night after the burning of the barn, four boys who had escaped from the Tilinava massacre ran through the grounds around my house. Two were between the house and the highway, and two ran through my garden. The two in the garden escaped safely but the others ran into the roadblock and were machine-gunned.

The Russian police put these two dead boys in the yard of Mr. Indriunas in the next village. They were left there ten days in the hot sun. Every day the farmer went to the police and begged them to remove the bodies. It became impossible for his family to stay in the house, but he was afraid to move the bodies. Finally, the police came and buried them in the flower beds near the house. About a month later these bodies were stolen, presumably by the boys' parents or relatives.

My next-door neighbor and good friend, Mr. Krivickas, had three sons. When the police came to arrest them, two escaped and joined the partisans. The eldest one was a teacher. When the police returned to arrest him, he managed to escape and joined the partisans too. The Russians suspected what had happened but weren't sure. One day a young partisan was killed and recognized as Krivickas' son. The next Sunday morning the Russian police came, searched their house and my house as well. Then they went to our church which was only a quarter mile away, forced the congregation to go to Krivickas' yard and ignited his house and his barns and stables with everything left inside; they told the people to see how the houses of partisans burned.

They arrested the father, but as Mrs. Krivickas was away from home she escaped immediate reprisal. Two days later, she came home to find no place to live. I saw her sitting silently on a stone in the yard surrounded by ruins and ashes. Heartbroken, I let her stay with me for a few days. She never complained, just repeated over and over again, "My poor children, my husband." I had no strength to comfort her. Then she went to live with some remote relatives, and eventually I was investigated by the police because I had taken her in.

To everyone's surprise, Mr. Krivickas was released after a few months. We couldn't understand why he hadn't been executed or deported. We all suspected a trick and wouldn't accept him into our houses. He would be given some bread or meat and told to go away. Later, in Novostroika, a good friend of Krivickas' and mine told me through tears how hard it had been for him to send Mr. Krivickas away. He felt even worse when he told me the story for he had been deported anyway and what worse could have happened to him if he had given that poor man shelter when he needed it so badly? Mr. Krivickas, over seventy years old, died on the road during the cold month of October.

The partisan situation steadily became more desperate. The Russians issued a few amnesty calls but those who responded were tortured until they informed on their friends and gave the locations of the hide-outs. That method also soon ended in failure.

The Russian police and specially assigned Russian Army units who were fighting the partisans persecuted everyone suspected of supplying the fighters with food, but when the partisans arrived at a farmer's asking for food he couldn't refuse even if he wanted to; if he did the *partisans* would persecute him.

I was in constant danger. One night in the winter of 1947 one of Krivickas' sons came to my window and asked again about news from America. He said that over a dozen partisans were sleeping in my small flax barn and I was to bring them some food. I cooked a big pail of soup and very cautiously took it to them, begging them not to stay long. They remained there all the next day. In the evening they moved out, which was a good thing because a few hours later a big detachment of Russian soldiers came to my house asking about the partisans. Perhaps someone had reported them. The soldiers searched and found nothing, not even a trace. Nevertheless I was arrested, taken to the nearest police station, interrogated closely and accused of harboring such enemies of the state as Mrs. Krivickas. I told them I was not capable of seeing an elderly woman sleeping, unsheltered, in the ashes of her home. They released me but I knew now that my life was not safe.

A new, more severe agrarian reform was introduced. Though under the new laws I was entitled to keep thirty-seven acres, I refused even this land and kept only the house and eleven acres. I had a cow, a pig, a sheep and ten hens and so managed to survive. For this amount of land and animals, my quota to the state was about one third of all the milk, 120 eggs yearly, about two hundred pounds of meat each year, and several bushels of grain. The rules for delivery were very strict. If a farmer did not fulfill the milk quota his cow was seized. If he did not deliver the other products, he might be jailed. Life was hard, dull, and monotonous.

Fortunately, my husband received the letter which I had sent through the Georgian officer. I was receiving many letters from John but it seemed that those I mailed to him were not getting through. He started sending me a few dollars at a time through a bank and in this way he managed to get my signature returned and so was sure that I was still alive.

The money he sent was exchanged at the official rate of four rubles per dollar. Black market prices were very high. A doughnut, for example, cost at least eight rubles. My son was now in elementary school and could write a little so I dictated a letter for him to send his father, telling him that for two green pictures (dollars) we could buy only a doughnut and asking that he send us food instead of money. This letter went through all right. Once John sent me thirty-five dollars. The value of this after it was exchanged was so negligible that I refused to accept the check. The money was sent back to him and he understood my indirect message.

I had never ceased my struggle to join my family. On April 7, 1945, after the Communists returned, I went to the Ministry of Internal Affairs in Vilnius, the Lithuanian capital, to ask about the possibility of going to the United States. I was advised to wait until the end of the war. Two weeks later, when the war ended, I again applied for a visa. All my applications were accepted and I filled out innumerable questionnaires. At about the same time I received an official letter from America together with affidavits and was certain that these gave me a strong argument for obtaining entrance to the United States. But they made no difference.

It was very hard to travel. By direct line to Vilnius was about 140 miles but the trip took me a day and a half and sometimes longer. Traveling without a special permit was out of the question and it took lots of time and effort to obtain one on the black market or by bribery. Even by taking a roundabout route it was impossible to get on a train without bribing the conductor of the car.

In the fall of 1945 I became very sick. I managed to get a doctor who diagnosed my illness as acute pleurisy and said I must get to a hospital. A neighbor took me to the hospital at Birzai by horse carriage. The so-called hospital had no equipment. I was put to bed without bedsheets or blankets and no food was available. I was there for over a month and survived only because my sister lived nearby and brought me food and bedclothes every day. The doctors were unable to get medicine but by bartering some of my food stock I obtained it on the black market. My son stayed with a farmer friend near our home while I was away and friendly neighbors cared for my livestock.

The clashes between the partisans and Russian security officers continued. The partisans could no longer stand against the Russians so they went completely underground and spent their energies in punishing Lithuanians who cooperated with the Communist government and persecuting Russian officers sent into Lithuania. The partisans from families which had been deported, jailed, or massacred, turned their rage against Communist officials from Russia. Even today there are very few Russian settlers in rural Lithuania by comparison with the numbers in big cities where they took over the best of everything. It seems that even yet the Russians do not feel secure in the farming areas.

The dreaded deportations also continued. The deportation in 1947 during the Christmas holidays was even larger than the big one which had taken place in 1945, and among the victims were several of my friends. During this time I visited Panavezys, and again saw the familiar sight—the station surrounded by strong military detachments and big crowds of people. It was a cold day in December but many children of the deportees were without hats or socks. The poor families had not been allowed time even to clothe their children properly.

When a family was deported, almost all of their belongings were left behind. Usually a board appointed by the Communist government made a scanty list of the property which was later put up for public sale at very low prices.

The best items never appeared at the public sale, because the important Communist officers and collaborators had first chance. What was offered the public was junk, but even this was completely bought out because, since nothing was available in the regular market, the demand for goods was very large. From the second arrival of the Russian Army until 1948, I could buy nothing in the legal market except salt and matches.

I was glad to have enough clothing left from the old times to clothe Johnny and myself. I made clothes for him from old things of mine and the remnants of my husband's. This old clothing also provided me with a living. I had enough food from my garden and animals, but I didn't have enough to sell to get money for other necessities and there were always the obligations to the state which I tried to fulfill. I sold old clothing and household goods in the black market and in this way obtained enough cash to purchase, also in the black market, things I could not make or grow at home. It was easy to sell desirable goods in the black market, but very hard to find them.

My only dream was to join my husband. Since I had had no success in Vilnius, I decided to go to Moscow. In September of 1947 my opportunity came when the wife of a Russian officer put her ticket and permit to go to Moscow on sale in the black market. It was a first-class ticket and I paid two hundred rubles above the official price. I knew that without an official travel order it would be impossible for me to stay in Moscow but the sister of an acquaintance was married to a Russian and had lived there since 1918. My friend gave me a letter of introduction and when I arrived in Moscow I found her sister without being stopped. She was kind and let me stay in her home.

In the same apartment house lived a Russian who was a former employee of a Russian ministry in the West. He became interested in my story and was kind enough to take me to the Russian Federal Internal Ministry in his car. I went in alone although at this time I could not speak Russian fluently. When I inquired for the proper office I was immediately questioned about how I had arrived there and who had sent me. I told the truth and was threatened with arrest because I had come unlawfully and was staying without registration. I promised to return to Lithuania immediately and they allowed me to go.

Obviously I could not expect any help from Moscow, so instead of going directly home I decided to stay one day longer in order to visit the American Embassy. There I found the people friendly but they told me that they had no way to help me because I was not an American citizen. The Consul promised to make an inquiry about my case in the Russian offices, to have my name registered there and to help me as much as he could. So I went home.

Three months later I got a letter from Vilnius to come immediately with my son to the Ministry of the Interior. I again went through all the problems of traveling, which were even harder because Johnny was with me, only to find myself being photographed, questioned, and dismissed. I had no idea why they called me; probably it was in connection with the inquiry from the American Embassy.

In the spring of 1947 it was decreed that ten old rubles would be exchanged for one new ruble but that official prices would remain the same. After the money reform, black market prices dropped considerably but still remained three to ten times higher than official prices.

In spite of constant rumors that Lithuanian farmers would be forced to join collective farms, the government claimed that because of the special structure of the land, Lithuania would keep private farming. However, in the early spring of 1948, all private farmers were required to pay exorbitant contributions in money. The taxation on my farm was six thousand new rubles, an impossible sum for me to raise.

Then in May of 1948 came the greatest mass deportation to date. All the farmers who had previously had a good deal of land and were considered rich, or who had better houses or furnishings than the average, were deported to Siberia. No allowance was made for those who had paid the full contribution; it made no difference who had paid half or who hadn't paid at all.

Before the fatal day of May 22, 1948, I had been preparing to go to Riga with two friends, named Aukstuolis. The Latvian capital of Riga was almost fifty miles away, directly on the highway which ran near my home. By hitchhiking, we could get there and return with a minimum of trouble.

We had discovered that the black market in Riga was a better place to obtain clothing, shoes and other items of necessity and had a much more favorable exchange rate for our farm products.

Both of the Aukstuolis women left on May 20 but I postponed my trip two days so that I could bake bread for my small family.

4

Deportation

About four o'clock in the morning of May
22 I heard a knock on my door. My neighbor, Jonas Vaiginas, called to me to open the door because he had something
very important to tell me. I opened the door and froze with
fear. Behind him was a whole detachment of soldiers, about
thirty altogether, all with heavy weapons. In the yard a
machine gun had been set up. The officer pushed me aside,
went into the house and demanded my passport and my
milk delivery card. After he had looked over these papers,
he took a letter from his pocket and read in a monotonous
voice that the state had decided to deport me from Lithuania to other Soviet states because I had done harm to the
U.S.S.R. I asked him what I had done wrong. He said this
would be told me later.

After this official announcement he told me to hurry because I had only a half hour to prepare myself for the deportation journey. Awakened by the noise, my son started
to cry. I quieted him and told him to go dress himself because I had more than I could handle to get the most important things ready to go. He tried, but prepared as if to
go to school. A few minutes later he came into the room

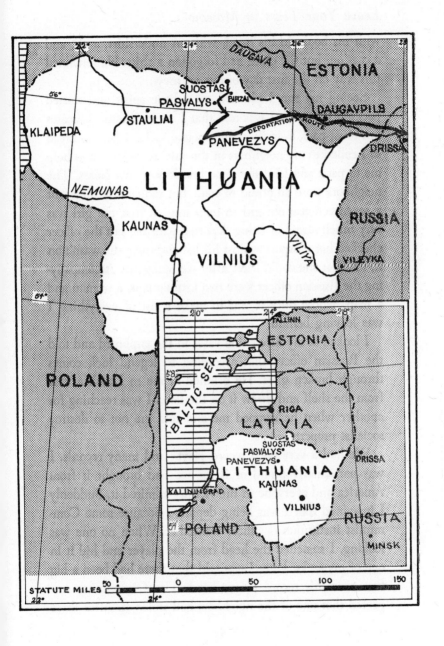

with his books in his hand, with an undershirt, a tie, and a coat on, but the child had forgotten a shirt. He remained this way on the first day of our journey.

Seeing my son I plucked up a little spirit and started packing like mad. I was told that I could take no suitcases but must pack everything into potato sacks. I had no bread so I called to my neighbors in the yard for someone to help me to pack and lend me some bread—just two pieces. The neighbors were all afraid to come but reluctantly they sent a seventeen-year-old girl to help me. At first the girl was very much afraid of being deported with me but the officer checked her passport against his list and since she wasn't on it, told her she could leave after we had gone. Accompanying the Russian officer were two Lithuanians, a woman and a man, whose duty it was to make a list of everything I was leaving behind.

I looked at my nice china vases in the cupboard and told the Russian officer that according to legend luck comes through broken glass. He grinned at me so I took a vase from the shelf and threw it on the floor. I was reaching for another when he stopped me and told me not to destroy socialist property.

We had a very good record player and many records. I was particularly proud of it for we had brought it from America and everyone in the vicinity admired it. Suddenly I imagined that I was being deported because some Communist institution or officer wanted it. When no one was looking, I snatched the head from the player and hid it in one of my sacks. Later I was told that there had been a big fuss over this record player head. The Communists suspected that one of the neighbors had stolen it. After three months in Siberia I got a letter asking where it was hidden. I wrote back saying that if they would send me five pounds of lard maybe I would tell them. Later another head was found in Riga and even today this record player is used in the Red Corner of a local Communist youth center.

I was able to get everything I thought was most important into sacks. Later I realized I had left many things behind which would have been invaluable, such as a clock, but I had remembered to take about six pounds of salted butter and about ten pounds of lard.

When the half hour was up, my son, myself, and our belongings were put into a buggy and escorted under heavy guard to the neighboring village of Suostas and put into a barn owned by Mr. L. Vaiginas. Mr. Vaiginas and his family were ordered deported and had been sitting there for most of the night. About three hours later, after some twenty-five families had been collected, we were sent, in the same buggies and with the same guards, to a village called Medeikiai four miles away, where we were kept for about four hours in another barn. All the roads were crowded with heavily guarded transports.

Each family sat on their sacks in a group. No one talked. When a new family came in, we all turned our eyes and motioned to them if they were acquaintances. Some women cried loudly at first but soon quieted. One of our neighbors, Mrs. Obeliunas, somehow persuaded the guards around the barn to allow her to come inside to me and hand me two hundred rubles. I had invested all my cash in eggs and butter for exchange in Riga, where I had hoped to find shoes for my son. The money was much appreciated but I was even more moved by her daring.

Some two hundred families had been collected and at about four PM we were put into trucks, each guarded by four Russian soldiers with guns. These trucks were nearly all American Lend-Lease equipment. We were taken to Panevezys, the largest city in northern Lithuania. The road to Panevezys led through the township of Pasvalys, where my sister lived. We stopped for a short time near my sister's house. She caught sight of me and gave something to her ten-year-old son to bring to me. He ran towards us but just then the trucks moved out.

After leaving Pasvalys the road passed my native village. Looking at the lovely old house where I had spent my happy youth, I burst into tears. I wondered if I would ever see my native village again, how long we would live, what future there could be for my son. . . . We had been horrified enough by the deportation of our friends and acquaintances, but it was quite different to experience it ourselves.

As we passed through a cemetery Mrs. Vaiginas started to sob loudly because her partisan son was buried there. I knew this but the others didn't and although they asked her why she was crying, she was afraid to tell.

At first I thought that all Lithuanians were being deported. In our wealthier neighborhood at least one family out of eight was taken. The village of Aukstuoliai, about three miles away from us, was left completely empty.

At the railroad station we were put into cattle cars, about forty to sixty people to a car. In each car there were two rows of sleeping berths but no mattresses or toilet facilities. People and their sacks of belongings took up so much room that it was hard to move around and there was hardly room to sleep—we were almost like herrings in a barrel. Even now I tremble when I remember it.

Mrs. Petrauskas, who lived two miles from my house in the village of Uzusiliai, was on the train. Her husband was in prison for political activities, leaving her alone with an eight-year-old daughter and a five-year-old son. When the deportation came she tried to commit suicide by jumping into their well but she was fished out with only minor scratches. She had been sent still wet to the barn with us, her children crying and no goods in her hands because she had wasted her time when she should have been preparing to leave.

In my car was the Tamosiunas family. When the deportation squad came, they found only the husband and a six-year-old child at home. The mother was in a hospital for the birth of another child. The soldiers snatched her and the new baby from the hospital only four hours after birth and put them into our crowded car. A widow about sixty-five years old had been living with her eighty-three-year-old bedridden mother. Her son was in prison. These women were also put into our car.

My friend Peter Dravinskas, his wife and two young children, were also there. Another friend I have already mentioned; Vaiginas, his wife, his mother, eighty-two, two daughters, fourteen and twenty-one, and a son.

The train stood in the station at Panevezys for two full days. We were given no food, only water for drinking and we could go out, with a guard, only for physical needs. Once we heard a woman crying in the second car from us. We were told she had with her a six-year-old son, and when the deportation team came her daughter had been injured by a machine gun while trying to escape. The girl had been taken to a hospital and her mother didn't know what would happen to her. The woman's husband had died in prison during torture while undergoing an investigation.

Our transport consisted of sixty cars so it can be estimated that it contained about 2,400 persons. Finally, the train started to move slowly. The people on the train and their relatives surrounding the station broke into loud weeping. Some youths in the cars began to sing Lithuanian patriotic songs. Some even sang songs of the partisan groups for they were no longer afraid. What worse could happen to them?

The feelings of human beings herded into cattle cars are impossible to describe. No one knew where we were going or what could be expected in the future. No one thought that we were to be killed, but no one knew how long we could survive. The misery in the crowded cars and the nervous tension caused by such a disaster could be compared with cattle being transported if they had intelligent minds. But even this comparison is not real, for such cruel transportation of cattle is forbidden by law in any civilized country. I think that if the Communists had done nothing more brutal than this kind of deportation, they still would have no right to be part of human society.

When I compared what I had been told about the method of deportation in 1941 with that which was applied to me, I found nothing had changed. Although it did not happen in my transport, I know from others that when a baby was born in a crowded car, no help was given. Even if there was a deported doctor or nurse in an adjoining car, they were not allowed to help because the rules said that in no case could an occupant of one car be allowed to move to another.

My two friends, Ona and Maria Aukstuolis, came back from Riga to find their houses empty and their families deported. Everything had been taken. These poor women remained in hiding for almost three years. Ona's husband and their daughter, and Maria's husband and two daughters were on our train.

There were some accidents. The train, after one day's travel, was going slowly through the Latvian forests towards Russia. A man and his two adult sons jumped off and hid in the forest. Guards sitting on top of the cars saw them and began to shoot. The train stopped for a few hours and we heard shots in the forest but the men were successful in escaping. Later, in another car, a woman with two small children whose husband was in prison, went mad, jumped from the moving train, and was killed. The train stopped and the woman was buried near the tracks. Everyone was talking about the poor children, only two and four years old, and we wondered who would care for them.

The train stopped a few times each day, sometimes in small stations, sometimes out in the fields. We were allowed to step outside but not allowed to cross the ditches on either side of the tracks. People had to take care of their physical needs under such circumstances. Men, young girls and women were side by side. Each time the train stopped in the vicinity of a Russian Army barracks, the train crews were sent to bring food. This happened sometimes once a day, sometimes every second day, so the passengers had to draw on the supplies they had brought from home.

The biggest problem we had was trying to take care of

the sick and the babies. In my car there were three babies. Their parents had great problems with diapers since it was impossible to wash them regularly. Sometimes when the train stopped after a rain the mothers would jump out to wash diapers in the ditches. There were fights over these water ditches because some wanted to wash dishes, some to wash their faces, while others wanted to wash dirty diapers, all at the same time. It was a little better when the train stopped in the larger stations where washing facilities and water were available. The parents made every effort to keep their children clean. Used diapers were dried and shaken out. Sheets and shirts were torn up to improvise diapers and sometimes the men tied the wet diapers around their waists in an effort to dry them more quickly.

The biggest problem on our car was our eighty-three-year-old paralyzed lady. There was no way to keep her clean. Very soon everything around her was stinking and she was covered with open sores. There was absolutely no medical care available. In some cars no doubt there were doctors, nurses or medical students, but they were not allowed to move.

Some days were very hot, the heavy smell in the cars was unbearable and a number of people fell sick. In our car one two-year-old boy ran a high fever and cried constantly because of pain. The only help his parents could get was a little aspirin which someone gave them. He grew worse and worse and finally died. At the next stop in an unknown forest the soldiers took his body from the train and presumably buried him. The sorrow and helpless rage of his parents was heartbreaking. Under normal conditions and with medical attention, he would not have died. Now, no one even knew for sure where he was buried. I was so thankful that my son stayed well.

Many wild rumors were circulated about our destination. The men who could speak Russian tried to question our guards, but they either said that they didn't know or else that they were not allowed to tell us.

We started the second week of our journey. Everyone was dirty and very tired. We heard that already about fifteen had died on the train, but our old paralyzed lady was still with us. We passed by, or met in stations, other big trains full of Lithuanians. We shouted to each other, asking where they were from. From the names of the stations we passed through we found that we were already behind the Ural Mountains going into Siberia; we were on the famous Trans-Siberian track. After about fifteen days we stopped in a station called Cheremkhovo. This place on the Trans-Siberian Railroad is about 160 miles from Irkutsk, the largest city in Siberia, near Lake Baikal. Someone knew that there were coal mines in the vicinity and we all thought that we would be put to work there.

We were kept on the train nearly twenty-four hours longer. On June 7 we were ordered to get out and stand on the platform. We stood there for about four hours in a cold rain mixed with snow. The children cried all the time. We glanced at the city a little and it looked very muddy and had no paved streets.

Later a Russian officer came and told us that we must take our things and put them into a barracks about a quarter of a mile from the station. He warned us to be careful because there were many thieves around. After that we were allowed to go to a bathhouse. This helped us immensely after two weeks of dirt.

After bathing we were ordered to stay near the barracks with our things and we were divided into three companies, according to how our goods were lying. Again there was much crying and yelling because each family wanted to go with their friends or relatives. The separation was made regardless of our wants and our protests made no difference. One third of the people were to stay in Cheremkhovo, another third was sent to Talniks to the timber industry, and the last third, in which I was placed, was sent about sixty miles from Cheremkhovo to Novostroika, another area of the timber industry.

The roads were very bad. We left after noon and didn't arrive until just before midday the following day. That night we slept in open trucks in the rain. The children were still crying and we did what we could to cover them up and comfort them.

In the morning we came to a river which had a small ferry. First the passengers were transported, then our goods, and finally the military trucks were taken across one by one. From this river it was about an hour's ride on a bumpy road to Novostroika. When we arrived the commandant of the place counted the people and became very excited because one was missing. Now we remembered that during the commotion at the river, our sick, paralyzed old lady had been left behind. An open truck was sent back to bring her, but the jolting and exposure were too much. She died just after arrival. Hers was the first Lithuanian grave in the Novostroika cemetery.

5

Novostroika—the Forest Village

ABOUT 130 FAMILIES arrived in Novostroika that day. We found the place very wild and run down. There were some barracks with broken doors and windows and about five new small houses. This was the "newer" section where the Russian administration lived, the camp commandant, officers, engineers, supervisors of the work teams, and tractor station.

When the trucks stopped our people started to get out and gather their sacks about them. I was in the last truck and while we were awaiting the order to get out the trucks were commanded to move on. We all cried and begged not to be separated from our friends and relatives, but no one listened. Fortunately, we drove only about a mile to another part of Novostroika called Gorodok. This was an older part of Novostroika, located directly on the Biela River, which is a very fast and noisy mountain stream coming from the Sajen Mountains. Gorodok was even more run down than the newer section. About ten families, mine included, were put into the schoolhouse. This was a one-room affair and we had hardly enough space to put down all of our sacks. There was no place to sleep except on the

floor and we cooked our meals out in the yard on improvised campfires. We remained there until school started in September and were very fortunate that there was little rain that summer. Directly above my area in the schoolhouse was a leak in the roof which soaked everything I had when it did rain.

The day after our arrival the camp commandant, whose name was Katshergin, came and ordered us to sign a paper which stated that we were banished to this place for the rest of our lives and that any attempt to escape would be automatically punished by a ten-year prison term.

We had time on the second day to look around a little. We found one store which had only rationed bread, matches, and salt for sale. Some Russians who lived there told us that in 1942 a few hundred families of Volga Ger-

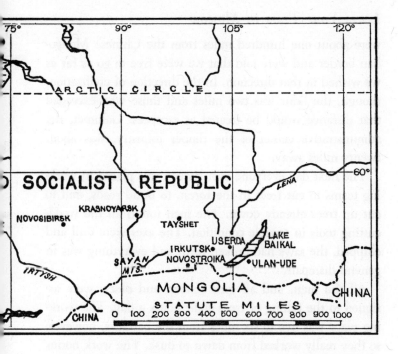

mans had been brought in but most of them had been taken away a week before our arrival; there were only two or three truckloads left. The big cemetery with German inscriptions on the wooden crosses told us the story. The Russians also said that twenty years ago their parents had been brought there with their families and left without any facilities for living. Only a few had survived.

It was now clear to everyone that we had been sent here to die. Some even said that we had been wrong to be so horrified by the Jewish massacre at Pasvalys. It seemed to us now that their execution was more humane than the suffering, exhaustion, and malnutrition which lay ahead of us.

As we looked about us we saw mountain slopes covered with huge evergreen trees in varying shades of green. We were about one hundred miles from the Chinese Mongolian border and were told that we were free to go as far as we wished in that direction. In the direction of civilization, though, the limit was two miles and those who exceeded that distance would be treated as escapees. Galumet, the administrative center of the timber industry, was about twenty miles away.

The next day everyone over sixteen was placed in working teams to cut trees in the forest, to build roads, and to cut up trees already down. The men found all the wood-cutting tools in terrible condition. The axes were dull and chipped, the saws had broken teeth and everything was in general disrepair.

All the men, and all girls sixteen and older, were assigned to the felling of trees eight hours a day. The working place was five to six miles from the barracks, however, so they really worked from dawn to dusk. The work norms were very high and with such poor tools and no experience, the men made only between fifty and sixty rubles the first month.

I was ordered to saw and split wood near the barracks. The trees were big and full of branches, and the women assigned to this task made only fifteen to twenty-five rubles a month, again because of poor tools and complete lack of experience.

A pound of bread in the store cost two rubles and the only way most of us survived the summer and the first winter was that we had supplementary food which we had brought from home. We had nice pieces of dress material, shoes, silver spoons, and so on which interested the Russians and they traded food for these items. After a month we were allowed to write letters home and soon began receiving parcels from relatives in Lithuania. The poor Volga Germans, who had already lived thirty years under Communism, had nothing left to barter and since entire communities had been deported they had no one left at home to appeal to for help.

The people of our group in the worst circumstances were those women who had many children and those who hadn't managed to bring enough good things from home to put them in a favorable bartering position. They were really starving. Poor women with children and without husbands formed a considerable part of our community. The Communists deported everyone that they suspected of not being loyal to their system. Naturally, women whose husbands were in prisons were liable to be considered untrustworthy.

I had brought with me a very good winter coat. When the opportunity came, I showed it to the wife of the forestry engineer, who was much impressed. I traded it to her for five hundred rubles, sixty heads of cabbage and thirty pails of potatoes. I was very glad to get the potatoes as there were none in the store and a small pail of potatoes was worth about eighty rubles, when you could get them from the local farmers.

I had an intense desire to let my husband know what had happened to us. Some time back, knowing that I might be deported, I had made arrangements with a friend working in a post office in Lithuania to immediately send a telegram to my husband that Barbara and Johnny had gone to visit his godmother. This telegram went through all right but later when friends of mine tried to write to John about me and send him my address in Siberia, they were not successful. I wanted to write to him myself but I didn't have a stamp and couldn't buy any. I wrote a letter anyhow and mailed it without postage and by some unexplainable set of circumstances it was sent on to him. I recently found it in my husband's file. It was written on poor paper and mailed in a dirty envelope, said very little really but did describe my feelings, so I repeat it here:

Siberia, July 14, 1948

Hello,

We arrived here one month ago. It's far from our native land—some 8,000 kilometers. Now I have even less hope of seeing you ever again. Our little Johnny is still alive, so am I. We are working in the woods on the construction of a highway. We are cutting down thick timber or pulling the trees out by their roots. There are quite a few Lithuanians here. Some of our common friends, among them: Indriunas, Aukstuolis, Dravinskas, to mention but a few. We, as well as the rest of the population over here, have a "very good life." We do not know for how long we will be able to remain alive. If you desire ever to see your Johnny again, help him as much as you can. Food is our greatest need. If you cannot send any food, please send money, it will help some. In the summer time we can buy milk here at a price of $2.00 a quart.

Big mountains and great forests surround us here. Good-bye to civilization—it won't be long before we find ourselves transformed to wolves. It's warm here in summer, but in winter the mercury drops to 50 below zero. They gave us a half hour to get ready for travel. You will understand that we were not able to take with us even the things we needed most. We are about 300 kilometers from the lake "Baikal."

I pray and hope that you will get this letter. Please

answer immediately and see what you can do about the food.

Barbara

P.S. I asked Johnny to add a few words to my letter, but he wants only some more bread which he is about through eating. Johnny and I are getting two pounds of bread per day and nothing else. Please, for heaven's sake, inquire whether you can send us some food.

By selling my overcoat to the wife of the chief engineer, I became quite friendly with her. I brought her some of my needlework as a gift. She was delighted with it and influenced her husband to get me a better job. I was appointed to be the cleaning woman at a children's home, similar to a kindergarten, for which I received 210 rubles a month. My duties were to clean the four-room house each day, help care for the children, and twice a week wash the floors. There was no soap available so I washed and polished them with gravel.

Children from two to seven years of age were accepted in this home, if their mothers worked. The women paid seventy-five rubles a month to have their children cared for and during the first years there were only twelve children, all from the Russian administration. The Lithuanian deportees had no money.

The food in the home was very poor. In the morning each child got a glass of tea with a little sugar in it and a small piece of black bread. For lunch there was a little potato soup with sometimes a bit of cereal to mix in it. At the end of the day they were given another glass of tea and another small piece of black bread with nothing on it.

55

I was very happy to work there because I made more money than in the woods and I was able to keep my son with me, although he was too old to be accepted, according to the rules. Occasionally the cook showed me a kindness and gave me a saucer of soup. The other women all envied me my good position.

At last we began to get letters from Lithuania and some lucky ones even got food parcels. Mail was delivered from Galumet once a week except in the spring and autumn when the roads were almost impassable. Then the mail was delivered once a month, by heavy tractors. From the letters we learned that the girl who had tried to escape and whose mother wept so bitterly in the car had died the following day. My friends wrote of the big celebration held by the Communists and their supporters after our deportation. There was plenty of poultry and other good things for a feast. No doubt they had all improved their standard of living by dividing up all that we had been forced to leave behind.

Here in Novostroika we had no electricity, no kerosene available to us, and no candles. We had great trouble in having any light at night. Some people tried using kindling, lighting one piece of wood after another. The more fortunate, who received fat from home, took a potato, scooped out the inside, filled it with fat, and made a wick from cotton threads.

The biggest problem for everyone was food. Once some butter was delivered to our store, at a price of sixty rubles per pound. There was only a limited amount but those who had money quickly bought out the stock, some using up a whole month's salary.

There were about 130 families in the Russian administration and a few free farmers and workers. Some of them had cows and many had gardens. Our people wondered why the Russians had such small gardens when so much fertile land was available; despite the short growing season, everything grew well and good crops could be harvested. Our farmers felt that if they were to live here as free people for a few years, it could be converted into a good place to live. Now, however, there was nothing and although at first the rate of exchange was good, later the Lithuanians had to offer more and more in barter and soon a nice gown was worth only a few potatoes.

In the summer many wild berries and edible mushrooms and nuts grew in the forests, but all the adults had to spend so many hours at work that they had no time to collect them. It would have been more profitable for us to gather food in the forests than to work but discipline was very strict and that was not allowed. Our children could do this kind of work but few families risked it. The forest was very big and wild. On their first trip two children got lost and when they were discovered two days later they were nearly dead. I never allowed Johnny to go at all.

Another problem we had was a lack of soap. For more than two years I didn't see a single piece of soap; not even the Russians had any. We had only water, sand, and ashes, and rediscovered laundering methods which had been used a thousand years ago.

We did have a medical officer. He didn't know much about medicine and his only duty was to write permits for people who were too sick to work. Anyone who didn't report for work and didn't have a permit was sent to jail for a few months. Among the deportees was a third-year medical student who knew a little more than the medical officer. He tried to help us as much as he could and even wrote back home for advice and asked to have books sent him. Even he could not help very much because no medicines or instruments were available.

Many of our workers, especially the inexperienced girls, were injured and sent to Galumet where there was a hospital and medical care. Children and other non-workers who fell sick were not sent to Galumet; they either survived, or died without help.

We were all weak from lack of food and the heavy work and long marches. We didn't spend much time thinking about better times. There were no books, only an occasional newspaper written in Russian which most of us couldn't read, and sometimes someone got a newspaper from Lithuania. These were our only contact with what was going on in the world.

As soon as we arrived, we tried to set up some kind of religious services. Some women had brought some saints' pictures but when we gathered together and started to sing, the camp commandant put a stop to it, saying that such gatherings were prohibited.

When it was time for school to start we were transferred from the schoolhouse to a barracks, but here was only more trouble. The barracks were old and infested with millions of bedbugs. We tried to fight them with boiling water, we tried calking all openings with lime, which helped for a little while, but soon they reappeared in hordes. Once I lost patience and decided to sleep on a table, first putting each leg in a container of water. Less than an hour later I was being bitten again; the bugs were dropping from the ceiling. After that we slept outdoors on our straw sacks or rolled in blankets. We asked the administration to do something but they merely shrugged their shoulders and said there had always been bedbugs in the barracks.

We were still very overcrowded. We had some cooking facilities but not nearly enough. More than half the people continued using open campfires all winter despite the intense cold.

Johnny started to school in September. They had a seven-year elementary school with three Russian teachers. Attendance was not compulsory and some people, angered by the all Russian vocabulary, kept their children home.

People in general began to adjust to the living conditions. We discovered that we were being cheated by the supervisor on the norms and tried to correct this situation. We found that the chief commandant was quite a drinker and could be bribed; by buying vodka for him many of us managed to find different and better-paying jobs. The men did everything possible to improve their tools. After they had sharpened and repaired them their salaries increased a little. Nevertheless, life was very hard. Very often the men went to work after having only hot water for breakfast. Each person carried a lunch of some sort. The administration did not care how you were dressed or equipped for work or whether or not there was enough food.

Autumn came quickly and it grew very cold. Many people suffered because they had had no time to bring heavy clothing from home and there was nothing for sale. According to our ration cards we were entitled to buy bread, fat, and meat products but we never had any meat or fat delivered to our store, except the one time I mentioned when some butter appeared.

Mrs. Bajorunas did not earn enough to feed her three children. She exchanged everything she possessed for food, even her blankets and pillows. She had only one dress left for herself and her children. When she couldn't feed her family any longer, she took all her children—seven, five, and three years old—and jumped into the river with them. She and all the children were fished out. After this she had a nervous breakdown and was sent to a mental hospital. It was pitiful to see the children. We all tried to help them but no one was able to do much. Filthy dirty, they crawled around begging for food, but somehow they survived. In a few months the mother returned. She then got a job cleaning the outside toilets and with the help of other people and by begging, she continued to live.

A similar story is about a woman named Vanagas who had two small children and was pregnant during the deportation. Her husband had been killed as a partisan. In the autumn she was allowed to go to Galumet for childbirth and due to complications she had to remain there about five months. The neighbors helped the children to survive. It must be said that during these times of greatest deprivation, all Lithuanians showed remarkable solidarity and helped each other in every way they could.

Not far from me lived another poor family named Vaitaitis. There were four children. The father had died in prison, after being tortured during an investigation. The mother had remained on the farm but as she could not deliver the required quota to the state she had been arrested. Only the children were deported, one a twenty-one-year-old hunchback girl, another girl nineteen years old, a thirteen-year-old boy and an eight-year-old sister. The healthy sister worked in the forest burning the branches as they were cut off. This job was very poorly paid and she made only twenty-five rubles a month. They hadn't known how to pack and had brought very little from home. I remember once seeing the crippled girl walk to a village to try to barter their last pillow for food. Despite help from the neighbors they sickened and became steadily weaker. The two youngest could hardly walk during the winter. Later the thirteen-year-old got a job washing the tractors in the garage but he was too feeble and after going to work twice he caught a cold and in six days died. The hunchback sister became sickly and swollen and died a few weeks later.

Our first winter came on very fast. The weather was fairly clear but very cold. In our barracks we had no clocks for the few we had brought with us had been exchanged for food. Since my work started very early, I soon learned to read time from the stars but when the sky was covered with clouds, I had trouble estimating the hour and a few times I started off to work as early as midnight.

The first Christmas approached. Our people gathered in small groups to sing our old Christmas carols in low voices because gatherings of large groups was forbidden.

We knew that we were at the bottom of humanity but we still enjoyed one thing—freedom to exchange opinions among ourselves without fear. I remember sitting together with a few friends who were better educated than I and discussing our fate. We were dirty, crowded, undernourished, and unbelievably tired. We wondered at the will for life which was still within us. It seemed remarkable that no one had gone insane or tried to commit suicide, except Mrs. Bajorunas. There were not even any criminal cases among us. We had been pushed back a thousand years in human civilization and achievement. One of the men said he didn't think that anywhere else in the world were human beings living so poorly as we.

Never had a state been given so much labor so cheaply. We were even financing the state enterprise with the little capital that we had brought with us. We exchanged our dresses, earrings, picture frames and silver spoons for food in order to be able to work and show results. The state octopus somewhere in central Siberia or Moscow was interested only in getting the most output at the smallest possible cost. What happened to the workers didn't matter in the least; we were virtually slaves; we were forced to work without regard to pay; we were put on jobs without our consent; we could not move from one barracks to another; and a permit was even necessary for us to go to the post office sixteen miles away.

In Novostroika there were a few educated Russians. We had three teachers in the school, two engineers, and some tractor-station operators, but it seemed that these people had no idea of human dignity. I remembered that in America and Lithuania we had always donated to people stricken by disasters, floods, fires, and earthquakes. We were now in worse condition than any of them but no one knew or cared about us.

People sat and wept for friends and relatives who were eight thousand miles away; for those who were in prison; and for those who had died in the hopeless fight for freedom. Everyone remembered the happy independent days before the occupation and we all talked about how we used to celebrate Christmas by going to church, decorating trees, and exchanging gifts.

The days passed in monotony. My job was always the same; at four in the morning I went to the children's home, brought water from the river in pails, chopped logs, and started the fires in the stoves. It seems ridiculous that, despite the huge forests around us, there was not enough wood for the stoves in the children's home. The woman supervisor of the home told me I must go and steal wood from the fences that people had around their gardens. I did this in the night for I was very much afraid that the owners would catch me and beat me but there was no other way—the children's home must be heated. All day I helped with the children, serving their food, maintaining order, and cleaning the rooms after they had gone home.

Each evening I cooked potato soup for our next day's meals. Before going to school, Johnny would warm the soup and eat some of it with one third of his bread ration. He was nine years old. I usually got home after sunset to find he had eaten almost all of his bread ration. I reheated our potato soup and sometimes enjoyed the luxury of putting in a small piece of bacon, for my sister had sent me a small parcel of bacon which was highly treasured. I was very careful with our food. The lard and butter which I had brought from home lasted for a full six months.

Besides the Vaitaitis children, my next neighbor in the barracks was Mr. Indriunas who had lived many years in Boston, saved money, and returned to Lithuania where he bought a farm in our neighborhood. He worked as a guard and took care of the horses. His wife worked on the ice road.

They used an interesting method to transport logs from the forest to the river. The roads were prepared in the summer, covered with water in the fall until they froze and became a solid sheet of ice. Then two parallel grooves were cut in the ice and sleds loaded with logs were hauled by tractors over this road with their runners in the grooves. It was important that the grooves or ruts be kept clear and so for each mile of road a woman was appointed to stay all day and clean the ruts of snow and pieces of ice. The work itself was not difficult, but it was hard to stay there all day in the subzero temperatures, and Mrs. Indriunas suffered extremely. I helped her to survive in the cold weather by lending her my felt boots. I had been fortunate enough to get a very good pair from the engineer's wife. Russian felt shoes cover the legs to just below the knee, are made of heavy felt, and are worn without rubbers in freezing weather. They are very light, warm, and excellent insulators. This pair had belonged to Mrs. Kalinin's husband and were a little large for me, but everyone envied me. Felt shoes are very important in this climate but they, like other necessary and desirable goods, were hard to obtain.

Mr. Indriunas apparently contracted anthrax from his work with the animals. His leg became swollen and gangrenous and the camp administration took him in an open truck to a hospital on one very cold January day. None of his family was allowed to go with him. He disappeared without a trace. His desperate wife and daughters asked the camp administration at every opportunity what had happened to him, but to no avail. A few months later, in

May, the camp commandant's assistant visited the Indri-unas family and told them that he had died a long time before. The family was never able to learn where he was buried.

After New Year's of 1949, one good thing happened to us. One day an announcement was made that bread was not to be rationed any longer and the price was to be dropped from two rubles to 1.75 rubles per pound. We told each other about this announcement with glowing eyes. There would be no hunger if there was enough bread. The bread of which I speak is not like the refined and bleached bread we have here in America. We could not have survived on that for very long. Siberian and East European bread is made of a rough-milled rye flour. It is hard and rough but retains all the vitamins and nutritious elements of the whole grain. Unable to believe that bread could be purchased without restriction, we bought up as much as we could afford and hoarded it. I prepared two big potato sacks of dry bread. Those sacks hung untouched for about two years until, feeling absolutely safe from the fear of a lack of bread, I fed it to my cow. I don't know how long we would have survived if the bread rationing had been continued. I felt such pity for those people deported in 1941. They had lived on one pound of bread per day for a full nine years and we nearly died in only seven months.

More good news came to me on February 16, 1949, when I received a notice from the post office in Galumet that a parcel from America was there for me. I went to the camp commandant to get a permit to walk to the post office to get my package. The news of this unusual event spread with the speed of light. People interpreted it as a sign that

the world after all did know where we were. I had many
volunteers to walk the sixteen miles and back to help me
carry the parcel, and one of my friends and I started off at
about midnight, pulling a sled. It was very cold and there
was a lot of snow. In the late evening when we got back
we found my entire barracks waiting for us.

When I opened the parcel, which weighed about twenty
pounds, many of the spectators were crying. They felt
somehow that this parcel was synonomous with freedom
and civilization. Everyone touched the small items, turning
them around and looking at the labels. During this and
the next day, the entire Lithuanian population of the camp
visited me. Some were so excited that they asked for the
labels from the packages and wrappings, which they hung
on the walls of their barracks. Even the wife of the commandant came to see my parcel and expressed the desire to
have all of the American cigarettes for her husband, agree-
ing to pay the price I asked. There were six packages of
Camel cigarettes in that parcel.

In the parcel were some fat, dried milk, saccharin, cigarettes, two pieces of material, a Boy Scout knife, thread,
needles, scissors, and other small items. I was very happy
with the food and completely delighted at the sight of the
material and sewing implements. We were not able to buy
thread so old pieces of clothing were unraveled to make
thread; it was a nerve-racking job. Very few had needles
and they were lent from person to person all the time. I
never knew before how much you can be annoyed by the
lack of a simple tool and how disastrous it is suddenly not
to have anything. In the local store we could not buy even
simple equipment such as pencils or paper. Many of the

first letters which went back to Lithuania were written on the bark of birch trees. Later our supply of paper came in parcels from home.

Spring was on the way and brought still more improvements. Some power saws arrived from East Germany and other good tools came from Czechoslovakia. The men increased their output many times. To our great surprise, the work norms remained the same and the men started to bring home five to six times more money than before.

There were elections coming up and we, as legal residents in the eyes of the law, were entitled to vote for various parliamentary offices. It was no surprise that we were perfect voters—one hundred per cent for the Communist Party candidates. Now when I read in the papers of Americans who have visited in Russia reporting that there everyone is happy, I think that if these people had come to our camp, even in the hardest times, and asked us in the presence of our camp commandant or his henchmen if we were happy, we would no doubt have answered that we were the happiest people in the world and were busily building a rosy Communist future. Somehow, the human being in a disaster condition fights to avoid falling into a worse state. Everyone wants to live a little longer and what is the sense in being tortured if there is any other way?

We started to prepare for the coming spring. Almost everyone asked the camp commandant for permission to establish vegetable gardens. There was plenty of land around which needed only to be cleared, mostly of tree stumps. By paying small bribes most of us obtained the necessary permission and when the frost was out of the ground we worked on Sundays and at night preparing the soil. The more active families who had adult sons and strong husbands made gardens covering over an acre of land. A woman like myself, without help, was able to cultivate only a small parcel. There were no horses or tractors available so we spaded our gardens with hand spades. The next problem was that we had no seeds to plant. Our folks at home sent us seeds for peas and beans and the Russians could hardly believe their eyes when they saw the well-cultivated plots growing good things to eat. Our gardens were a big help and the people felt more optimistic about the second winter.

I still worked in the children's home. I was happy that Johnny was one of the best students there and all the teachers liked him. My son and the other young Lithuanian children were very confused. The teachers ran the classes in the usual way using the standard Communist propaganda line about how good the Communist system was for the ordinary workers, how they weren't exploited, how all people in Russia now were free, and how the standard of living was improving all the time. The children couldn't reconcile this preaching with the facts as they knew them and the parental opinions which they heard.

Our people now asked the commandant and other officials to allow them to build new barracks and also a special barracks in the remote place in the woods where they were working. Walking six to ten miles every day to and from work was an almost unbearable task. Permission was granted and they started to build with enthusiasm, even spending Sundays on the project.

In the summer of 1949 our living conditions became less crude. Now only five to six families cooked on one stove.

But it was at this time we found that even being at the bottom of society did not assure us the luxury of opening our minds. Three of our men, Ausiejus, Briedis, and Locirius, were sent to Galumet for extra work in the early summer. Auciejus could speak very good Russian. He was the only one to return; both of the others were arrested and charged with propaganda against the government. For the first time, people were frightened and began to be suspicious. Perhaps someone among us was an informer. Everyone suspected Ausiejus and believed that the other two had been sent with him because they were already under suspicion.

We didn't know what had happened to them. Locirius was a bachelor but Briedis left an eighteen-year-old daughter and a seven-year-old son. His wife had not been at home at the time of the deportation and had been left behind. The daughter was living in the barracks in the woodcutting area and the son was left almost without care. He was too old to be accepted in the children's home and he wasn't eligible to go to a detention home because according to the law he had a relative, his sister, who was supposed to look after him.

Among the Lithuanian population there were many good-looking girls. All had gone to high school and some even to college at home. Now they were deprived of further study, though later on two girls managed to finish seven years of school in Novostroika and were given permits to go to a secondary school in Galumet. Perhaps more permits could have been obtained but it was expensive to supply a youngster with food and clothing away from the family. One girl, whose father worked as a bookkeeper in the administration, tried to get a permit to go to the college in Irkutsk.

All the local authorities agreed but it was refused by the higher-ups. It seemed as though it were the general policy to deprive our children of a decent education.

The men in the Russian administration liked the Lithuanian girls and one newly appointed engineer, a work dispatcher named Stipiagin, fell in love with Milda Aukstuolis, the daughter of my friend who had been in Riga during the deportation. At first he was very hard with all of us but when he fell in love with Milda he changed considerably. He wanted to marry her but the administration was against it. It was pointed out that he couldn't afford to marry anyone who had no freedom to move—proof to us that we were considered slaves.

I had begun to get parcels regularly and at last food was no problem. I even made money by selling materials which my husband sent me but, never being sure of the future, I still kept the better things from each parcel for the unknown dark days which might lie ahead. Nothing was certain, I could not know whether we would stay here or be moved, or how long I would be allowed to receive the parcels from John.

Again winter came and now we were all living a little better. In 1949 two babies were born in our community of 550 people. Drevinskas had a daughter and Pilkauskas a son. (Later the baby boy died.) Until the spring of 1951, when I was arrested, no more babies were born, so, despite improved conditions, the material and mental harshness was too great; our small community was dying off.

We already had many graves in the cemetery. One three-year-old boy had died in the past summer, and we were all saddened by the death of a lovely seventeen-year-old girl.

In the summer of 1949 she grew very thin, felt ill, and coughed constantly. Her parents suspected tuberculosis and begged the administration to free her from work in the forest. They were not successful. Since everyone was so thin the work supervisors were not impressed by her appearance and forced her to go to work every day. One Monday morning they found her dead.

The administration permitted some funeral ceremonies. The men made a big cross which was carried before the procession and there were lots of flowers from the forest and meadows. Almost all the Lithuanians of Novostroika participated in these funerals, singing our Lithuanian funeral chorals.

Winter came fast and in October the River Biela was half frozen over. A team of men and young girls was putting logs into the river, which would be washed downstream in the spring when the ice started moving. One day during the lunch break, a girl named Meskinis went to an open place in the river to get some drinking water. There were not enough wells in the village and usually we had to drink water from the river. The girl never returned. After a little while, the other workers investigated, found her footsteps in the snow near the edge of the ice, and decided that she must have slipped into the water and drowned. This was reported to the commandant and he was much concerned, not about the girl, but about the possibility that she had escaped. He appointed a fifteen-man crew to search for her body. The search continued all winter for a day or two each week. Finally in the spring her body was found washed down the river about thirty miles.

The commandant was much relieved and our cemetery in Novostroika had another new grave.

During the winter of 1949-50 I visited the forest barracks where the workers spent the weekdays. It was small and extremely crowded. There was one oven in the middle of the barracks on which each person cooked his own meals from the supply of food he had brought with him. It was interesting that the Communists, who are so very much in favor of community life, still preferred to have the workers feed themselves individually. A common kitchen would have been much more sensible. Everyone lived together in this one barracks, including many men and young girls. The men's wives and children were in the old barracks in the village. Many were not pleased with this splitting of families, especially the girls' mothers.

Still, life was better than it had been. Now that we had enough bread, and food from our gardens, we had money to spare for other things. The collective farms for many miles around got the idea that in the wood-cutting camps people had money. From nowhere, it seemed, there appeared various kinds of food, even sometimes meat which cost ten to fifteen rubles a pound. Our people were able to buy cows and thereby improve our nutrition, which was especially good for the children. Even I was able to buy half interest in a cow for a thousand rubles. It was a great comfort to watch Johnny growing strong at last and to see no more crying children always hungry and asking for bread. Also, we had built another school which was much larger than the old one so that the children were no longer crowded. Now all the children, both Russian and Lithuanian, were able to go to school although, of course, the classes were conducted in Russian only.

In the summer of 1950 the supervisor of the children's home left for Russia and another woman took her place. I had been on good terms with the first supervisor and she often got some things from my American parcels. The new supervisor was very much against me. The wives of the Russian officials had been conspiring against me because of my easy job as caretaker of the home. They felt that sort of work should be saved for Russians. I was now so well off economically that I could have lived on the income from my parcels but I would not have been allowed to do that. Everyone who was not sick or very young was forced to work, especially the heads of families. I was transferred to the building of a new road through the forest, working on a twenty-woman team. The work was extremely hard and we stood in water to our knees most of the time. We dug ditches, took out tree stumps and occasionally even felled trees. Because of the bad working conditions and our inexperience, our output was very low and I made only about forty-five rubles a month.

After working at this for two months I was again transferred, this time to a sawmill which had been built during the winter and was equipped with new machinery from East Germany. The mill provided good-paying jobs for our people so it was now possible to build new and better barracks. I worked on a circular saw. There were no cranes to transport the logs and it was the job of two women to take the cuts from the saw and pile them in the yard. This was a strenuous job and at the end of each day I was ready to drop, but I made five hundred rubles a month.

On November 8, 1950, while I was going to lunch, the news was spread that the secret police had come and arrested four men from our group. They were Strelciunas, Dagis, Kartanas, and one whose name I can't remember but he was a naturalized American citizen who had come back from the United States about a year before the war and bought a store in Pasvalys. They were whisked away. No one knew what had happened to them but after six months they were returned. There was a secret court held in the commandant's office at which all were sentenced to ten years in prison. After the sentence they were allowed to see their wives and children to say good-bye.

Eventually we discovered what technique was used in arresting people. We suspected that some spy system had been established by our camp commandant. Later the secret police came from the bigger centers and with the information supplied by these spies would try to make a case. They had secretly taken some from our colony and made them sign statements that they had been witnesses when someone spoke against the U.S.S.R. At first the "witnesses" refused, but when threatened that they could also be accused as enemies of the state, they succumbed and signed. Then they were warned that if they told about this they would be punished with at least five years in prison.

We noticed that certain people went many times to the commandant's office and never told us later what they had been doing there. After enough "testimony" was collected, someone would be tried as an enemy of Communism and sentenced. My friends, in commenting on these cases, felt that even here Russia was trying to eliminate any outstanding persons. All of those arrested were the leaders with authority and influence. It seemed that the Russians were trying to disorganize the deportee community, by leaving it without leadership, which they had done on a big scale in the whole of Lithuania. Others said that the apparatus of justice of the Russians was a fine-grinding machine which required victims or it could not survive. The job of the secret police and the courts apparently was to supply the victims. I thought that both theories were probably true.

It would not be right to imply that only the Lithuanian deportees worked under such hard conditions. The Russians were paid at the same rate we were. Some of these Russians were free and some the remnants of former deportations. There were even a few families of Crimean Tartars from the nation which had been exterminated and the few remaining people scattered through the country when Russia regained the Crimea.

Apparently our administration was under constant pressure to increase production and they tried always to get more workers even from among free Russians. Agents traveled across Russia promising good wages and living conditions and giving a bonus of one thousand rubles in advance to anyone who signed a contract to work one year in Novostroika. These poor Russians arrived totally unprepared, with inadequate clothing and no experience of work in the forests. Some families were so poor and dirty that we pitied them and supported their children. No one from these groups stayed more than a few weeks. They turned back; not being deportees they could do this. Some of them were later arrested for breach of contract and jailed unless they could return the thousand rubles advanced them.

Our living conditions continued to improve. The people now had money left over after the first necessities were paid for and so they started to drink. It was a shame to see that a large part of our male population got drunk every week end but, looking back, I can understand it. It was the only escape they could find from the monotonous hopeless life.

We became experts on the Russian way of life. We found that for any favor you must bribe the responsible official. Our commandant tried to increase his income by various methods. Once he announced that a photographer was coming and would make three pictures for each person. All the pictures were taken and we paid ten rubles each for them. We never saw the pictures or the photographer again, though we learned that he stayed in Novostroika a few days drinking with the commandant. I later heard that the commandant, Katshergin, was killed in a drunken brawl by a Russian deportee in Cheremkhovo.

In the winter of 1951 I again changed my job from the sawmill to being a messenger in the tractor station. In our tractor station there were ten tractors, each with an operator and an assistant. There was also a repair shop, with three mechanics and a welder. During the winter season the tractors worked in three shifts and if some mechanical failure occurred or someone was injured or suddenly got sick, the mechanics' or drivers' replacement had to be called out no matter what the time of day or night. Since there was only one telephone line in Novostroika, which connected the camp commandant with the Director of Works and the tractor station, a messenger was kept at the station at all times. There were two of us and we worked alternately in twenty-four-hour shifts. The settlers were scattered through an area about three miles in diameter and it was often necessary to walk through the deep snow in the forest at night a distance of two to three miles and back. I was always afraid on this job because the wolves were dangerous. I bought a lantern and carried it with me to frighten them away. The hardest time of all was on Monday because most of the men were drunk and were not interested in going to work, so I would have to visit them several times.

My situation was very good for I was still making five hundred rubles a month and was not always so tired as in my sawmill job. By our standards I became a rich woman. My husband sent me parcels regularly and I received them without restriction. In two and a half years I received twenty-five to thirty parcels which were very valuable. In 1949, also, I received letters regularly. We had no reason to hope for a reunion, but John always tried to be cheerful and said that somehow the situation would change and my life would not always be so hard.

In 1950 the letters became scarce. I received only four. All the others were held up, presumably by the secret police. After 1950 I received none at all. My husband received only the one letter which I have told of before. I tried everything I could think of but had no success, my letters all disappeared in the post office. I did manage to get word to him in a roundabout way, by writing to a friend in a Lithuanian city who sent telegrams to my husband about me, which he received. At least he knew that we were alive.

I was so glad that my son, now my only reason for living, was a good, serious boy and an especially good student.

6

The Journey to Irkutsk

ON APRIL 20, 1951, about ten in the evening, Johnny came to me at my work place and told me that I was to report immediately to the camp commandant. I went to him at once and he declared, "You will be sent to another place. I advise you to sell your cow and potatoes as soon as possible and pack everything."

I was frightened and asked if my son could go with me. I thought I was being arrested. He said, "Yes, you can take him," and then ordered me to tell no one that I was being sent away. How could I manage that? When I returned to the barracks and started packing, people asked what was happening and there was nothing I could do but tell.

I sold my potatoes easily but had trouble disposing of my cow. My partner, Mr. Januskevicius, refused to pay me for my half interest saying that he didn't have the money and would send it later. Under our living conditions, later meant never and I was very much concerned. After all, one thousand rubles was a lot of money. Another Mr. Januskevicius, not related to the first, who worked in the bookkeeping section of the industry, paid me the thousand rubles for my share. When he heard that I had obtained the money from a person working in the administration, my partner immediately agreed to pay me for the cow.

I worked all night packing. I had no idea when or why I was leaving and soon the inevitable rumors started. Even I believed the report that I was going to America to join John. Maybe he had been able at long last to help me.

During the next two weeks nothing happened. While I waited, I visited the camp commandant again, asking him about my destination but he would tell me nothing. A new batch of deportees arrived, this time families from the West Ukraine, and I was told to pack everything on one truck and use it on its return trip as my transport. There was a driver, his assistant, and a soldier who was to be my guard.

We left Novostroika after noon one day and arrived in Galumet, twenty miles away, at noon the next day. The weather was somewhat warmer and the roads were thawing and very muddy and bad. We spent the night, which was still very cold, in the open truck. My son had not felt well before our departure and now was running a high fever. I was terrified that this hard journey might be fatal to him. I asked both the driver and the soldier about my destination but they said they were not permitted to tell me.

Before we reached Galumet, an official riding a horse stopped us and asked if I was Armonas. It seemed that they were concerned about what had happened to me, I had been so long in getting to Galumet. This official concern was a great relief. I had noticed that my companions had been looking with keen interest at my luggage and was afraid that they might get rid of Johnny and me and divide our things.

After we left Galumet, the truck suddenly stopped and

the driver started throwing out all my luggage. He told me that he was to take Johnny and me but no one had said anything about my luggage. I negotiated with him and agreed to pay eighty rubles for the transportation of the goods. We stopped at the next village, while the soldier and drivers spent all that money eating and drinking.

I knew we were traveling in the direction of Cherem-khovo, but the road was so bad that we could only go one or two miles an hour. Evening came and again we were forced to spend the night in the open. It was drizzling rain and my son was very sick. I asked the driver and the soldier to help and promised to pay them more. In the distance we saw a light and the soldier agreed to carry my boy on his back. When we arrived at the lighted place we found a tribe of local Buriat Mongols. They agreed to keep Johnny overnight for ten rubles. I returned to the truck to make sure that my goods were safe.

The next day the truck got stuck many times and we worked hours trying to push it out of the mud. In the evening we crossed a small river and there the truck bogged down so thoroughly that we couldn't move at all. We spent still another night in the open. Not far from the river we saw an abandoned house so we went there, broke up some remnants of a fence, made a fire in the corner and tried to escape the bad weather which was especially hard on my poor little sick boy. The soldier and the drivers had nothing left to eat so I fed them from my supply.

The next morning we set to work to free the truck. We cut big tree branches and worked like mad but it didn't help. At midday we noticed that the driver's aide had disappeared. He had had enough. It was a pity we had such a mishap at just that point for a few hundred yards away there was a hard-surfaced road and we saw trucks passing by. The men realized that they couldn't free our truck so they went to the paved road to try to flag down another. After a few hours they were successful and the driver agreed to take me with all my belongings to Cheremkhovo for one hundred rubles. Since I was anxious to end the journey as soon as possible, I agreed to pay the required sum.

Now the driver and the soldier became my friends and helped me move everything from one truck to the other. It took us more than a half a day. The soldier came with me but the driver was responsible for his truck and was afraid to leave it so he stayed behind. He had nothing to eat so I again gave him food from my store of American goods.

This was the fourth day of travel. The new driver took us only to the outskirts of Cheremkhovo and then said it was illegal for him to carry passengers; we would have to get out. The soldier left me alone and went to the city for help. Six hours later he came back with a truck and once more I had to pay for transportation.

The soldier now revealed the secret of my destination, telling me that I must continue my journey to Irkutsk by train. He said that near the station he had an aunt and he thought we could rest there. No one had told me about the train trip before so all my things had been incorrectly packed; no railroad would transport them. The soldier's family was friendly but lived very poorly and when I started unpacking my goods their eyes opened wide. I made a bigger impression on them with the goods from my luggage than a Continental convertible would make in the most remote American village. Immediately the aunt prepared a good meal from my American canned goods and just as quickly relatives and friends assembled to see this marvel. I was so exhausted that I could only look helplessly on while they inspected all my things. I was amazed that very few items disappeared.

When I started repacking, I found that only about a third of my things could be taken with me. I left the remainder with the aunt for her to keep until I could return but, needless to say, I never went back. My soldier guard turned his responsibility for me over to another soldier from the commandant's office in Cheremkhovo and told me that he had no food or money to return to Novostroika so I gave him money for the final time.

I arrived in Irkutsk with only small handbags, all my other things being in the baggage car, and my guard took me to a cellar which was used as an intermediate station for deportees. This shattered all my hopes because I felt that if I were to be permitted to go to America, they would have treated me differently.

After being there for two hours, another soldier came and we went about two miles on foot to the deportee commandant for the city of Irkutsk. After the personal information about me had been taken down, we began walking again, this time to our new living place, about three miles away. I was so tired and my son was so weak that we could barely make it. Even the soldier noticed our condition and carried my small luggage so that I could help my son to walk. He was now too big to carry.

7

The Irkutsk Jurta

WE WERE TAKEN to a terrible slum on the outskirts of Irkutsk. Our housing was in the so-called "Buriat Mongolian Jurta." Jurtas are round barracks about thirty feet in diameter which have a stove in the middle, an entrance door and many radial partitions about head high. They had previously been used to house Japanese prisoners but now only Lithuanian and Volga German deportees were housed in a colony of fifteen such structures.

In the jurta to which we were assigned lived four Lithuanian families. One was the Buzys family. Mr. Buzys was in a Lithuanian prison, but the sick mother, one daughter, Ona, nineteen years old, a younger daughter, and a small son lived together. Originally they had been deported to a Buriat Mongol collective farm where conditions were horrible and they had to sell everything to keep themselves from starving. Later they were transferred to this settlement. Now Ona worked in a supervisory position and her sister had a part-time job so the family managed to exist.

Another large family, named Doleris, occupied almost half of the jurta circle—the father, mother, a grown son, and three daughters. The oldest daughter, Helen, was a handsome young woman but somehow didn't look honest to me. This family had been deported first to a collective farm and later lived in the gold mining area of Badeibo, where there were many Lithuanian deportees. It seemed that all Siberia was populated with Lithuanian deportees. The people in the gold mines lived better perhaps than others because despite strict controls they still managed to steal a little gold which they exchanged on the black market for food.

The third family, the Marinskas, had owned a large farm in Lithuania near Vabalnikas. The older daughter worked on the building of new street-car lines, the boy on the construction of new houses. The mother didn't have a regular job but she made fair money doing housework for the Russian high officials.

There was a small section in the jurta in which lived a mother and her two children, a daughter of ten and a son of eight. Her husband was not at home at the time of her deportation and was left behind. He worked now in a hospital in Lithuania and managed to send them food parcels. The mother worked at road building for three hundred rubles per month.

I was squeezed into the same room with this woman, whose name I have forgotten. She was very unfriendly and cursed me all the time as though it had been my idea that I should be there. No one gave me any furniture so we slept on the floor for a week until I found an iron bed in a pile of garbage. I found a Lithuanian craftsman who for two cans of American meat fixed the bed so we could sleep in it. When I brought my bed into this jurta section, there was no room left for the table, which had to be moved when anyone wanted to go to bed. The situation became worse when my luggage arrived from the railroad station. The only place to store all of this stuff was under the table, and when I needed to open my luggage it was necessary to put the table on top of my bed.

The day after my arrival I was taken to my job on the construction of a new house. Almost all the workers were Lithuanian and Volga Germans and they were all deportees. It was a big building but there were no cranes available. I was one of the workers who carried the heavy materials such as brick, mortar, and sacks of cement to the third, fourth, and fifth floors. I was paid three hundred rubles a month. However, even given the opportunity, I seem unable to work slowly, so as usual I worked hard and intensively, which was noticed by the officials, who treated me quite kindly.

The most troublesome part was the walk to and from work. Since I lived on the opposite side of the city from the construction site, I had to travel an hour and a half on the street car and then walk two and a half miles, which took me another hour and a half. I felt that my whole life was spent in traveling back and forth and working. A Lithuanian who was night watchman of the construction showed me an old tool shack. It was very small but I thought how happy I would be if I could live there. The management agreed to allow me to use the shack. It was almost a dog house, to live in, but when I asked our camp commandant for a transfer he became violently angry and yelled at me and said no. I was very uneasy after this happened, because I had been told he was an even-tempered man.

The city of Irkutsk made quite an impression on me after living in the wilderness for three years. Even in our shabby and run-down jurta which was infested with bedbugs, we had an electric light. In the evening I was free to attend the various entertainment places such as the movies or theaters. My life was not restricted so long as I went to work, didn't try to change my living quarters, and didn't try to run away. The only prohibited place was the railroad station.

Through this transfer, my son lost about a month of school, and it was time for examinations when we arrived in our new place. He was still weak from his illness and I couldn't take as good care of him as I wanted because I had to be away all day. To my surprise, he passed his examinations with above-average grades.

I wrote my husband a letter telling him where we were and that we were back in civilization but living worse than we had in Novostroika. I missed my friends whom I could trust and whom I had known during the terrible deportation and the first year of hardship.

The two young women, Ona Buzys and Helen Doleris, however, were very sociable. Two weeks after my arrival they gave a party in our jurta and invited me and many other Lithuanians. There were about twenty-five there, mostly younger people. Each of us donated ten rubles towards the cost of the party and there was plenty of vodka. The young people danced and sang Lithuanian songs. With the vodka for support, their boldness increased and they started singing a new song composed by the deportees which ran, "Who lives in shacks and runs around in rags, will never conquer the world."

Life in Irkutsk in May of 1951 was difficult. There were few products available. You could buy only very expensive canned meats. There was no fat at all and the longest lines were always for sugar. Some of the youngsters were professional line-standers; for two or three rubles they would take your place in the sugar line.

In May we were allowed to plant potatoes in gardens in another part of the city. It was hard to get potatoes at this time. I had to pay 150 rubles for two pails of them to plant. Later, when we visited the potato garden we found the soil was so poor that we would have almost no harvest. I remember saying, "This damned Siberia—even potatoes won't grow here."

Life was terribly monotonous. Since I spent nearly all my time at work, I was very much concerned about my son. He had already made friends with different boys and had even gone boating on the big Angara River. I didn't feel that all the people in our jurta were trustworthy. They were different, and I didn't think they were fit to care for Johnny.

One day a young Lithuanian named Kunigelis visited us with a camera and wanted to make photographs. Helen Doleris persuaded me to stand in front of our jurta with her and have our pictures taken. This apparently insignificant event was to acquire importance for me in the future.

On July 24 at five in the morning someone knocked at our door. We opened it and found three secret police cars standing outside. Three or four men came into each jurta and searched everything. They looked very carefully through my things, took some of my letters from Lithuania, some letters from John, and a few pictures. I thought I would be arrested immediately after the search so I quietly gave my son all my money. After they finished the search, they made some remarks about the good things that I had, and then left. Three days later the assistant to the commandant came and made a list of where we each worked and what we did and declared again that anyone who tried to run away would automatically get twenty-five years at hard labor. A week later they arrested Ona Buzys, kept her all day, and later released her. She came back but didn't say anything about what they did with her. After this another young girl was arrested and later released. So, one by one, a large part of the jurta population was taken away for investigation and returned afraid to say what questions had been asked.

During this period a mother of two small children was arrested. Two days later her husband was arrested but, surprisingly, after two more days both were released. When she came back she was not afraid to talk even though they threatened to imprison her for ten years if she did. She said she was asked about Miss Lapinis, a nice girl living in another jurta, and about me, and others. They tried to get out of her various small accusations against us, threatened to arrest her and send her children to a detention home. She denied everything; yet they released her. She told us that anyone who agreed to do everything they asked got good food from the officers' kitchen. Because she and her husband would not cooperate they were fed from the prisoners' kitchen. Now we knew how everyone behaved because even though they wouldn't tell what they were asked and how they cooperated, they would tell how they were treated and what they ate; and that told us enough.

Almost everyone was caught up in the investigation now except me and about ten others. We knew something was definitely wrong but still didn't know what. I was not so much afraid for myself as I was for Johnny. He was my only hope, he was all that kept me going.

I had over two thousand rubles and many good things from my American parcels and tried to think of a way that I could secure my wealth for my son in case of my arrest. I knew one very trustworthy woman, who was a tailor. I gave her a thousand rubles to keep to use for Johnny in case I was arrested but three days later she brought the money back to me saying simply,

"I am afraid."

I tried another good and serious family but they were also afraid and refused. I knew there were many people who would agree to take care of him but I didn't trust them because I knew they were interested only in the money and goods and wouldn't give him help when he needed it.

In desperation I took two thousand rubles and sewed them into the shoulders of my son's overcoat. I squeezed two hundred rubles into the soles of his shoes. I tried to talk with him and explain what he must do and how he must behave if I disappeared, but he didn't take me seriously. I told him about the hidden money and warned him not to tell anyone but to keep it to himself and use the money only in an emergency.

Our position with the inhabitants of the jurta was exceptional. I was considered a very rich woman and I remembered the big eyes my roommate made when she saw my hoarded goods from the parcels as I unpacked them after they came from the railroad station. Everyone knew I had good American canned meats and other delicacies. There were too many people for me to share my goods with all of them and there was much envy shown.

After our house was searched three weeks went by and still nothing happened. Everyone became calmer. Sometimes after work I met my son in the city and we went to the movies. The center of Irkutsk looked fairly prosperous, but the suburbs were real slums. The people were not bad, but quiet and suspicious. I never became involved in a conversation with a Russian. From former experience I knew that one thing a Russian will never discuss with you is politics.

It was a different story while we were at work. I had an interesting talk with a Russian-born German. He had worked in western Russia, was taken by the Germans and later worked in Germany. Since his whole family was in Russia he had decided to return to them. Now he cursed this decision. As he passed over the border, everything he had was taken from him. He was sent to work in the coal mines in the Ukraine and was later transferred to Irkutsk as a deportee. He had never seen his relatives.

I was still preparing for the dark days which I felt sure were coming. I sent a parcel to my sister in Lithuania and also sent her three hundred rubles.

8

The Arrest

On August 29, 1951, my son was still asleep
when I left for work at seven A.M. At lunchtime I decided
to go to the market to buy something for dinner and had
reached the street car when I heard,

"STOP."

I turned and saw our chief camp commandant and one
of the men who had searched our room. They told me to
follow them and we went to a parked automobile where
they read out the warrant for my arrest. I asked if I could
go home to get some things and say good-bye to Johnny
but they told me that I had seen enough of my child, and
with that we drove to the prison.

At the same time the eight men and the other women
who had been left alone so far were arrested at their places
of work on the railroad and at construction sites. None of
us was allowed to go home. When evening came and so
many people didn't come back, everyone in the jurtas knew
what had happened and there was much excitement. I was
later told that my eleven-year-old son cried all night but
everyone was afraid to try to comfort him. He was alone
for over a week and lived on things from our canned stores.

Among those arrested was Leonavicius, an only son of elderly parents, who was sentenced to twenty-five years. His father broke down under shock and was sent to a home for the insane. His mother died a short time later. Kubilevicius, Lapenas, and Stase Valeckas were all under twenty-five years of age and all sentenced to twenty-five years. Mrs. Stremikis was forty and received a twenty-five-year sentence. Kunigelis was sentenced, mostly for the unlawful possession of a camera and the taking of photographs, to ten years. He was eighteen at that time. Another woman got ten years, leaving her husband and a seven-year-old son.

None of them could understand why they were punished so severely. None had resisted the Communist regime, none belonged to secret organizations, or had sabotaged their work or had done any other unlawful deed. They had, however, openly expressed their complaints about their hopeless situation and perhaps told a few things about their torturers. It was a sadistic absurdity to punish these proud Lithuanian farmers because they were unhappy in their status as the lowest class of Russian slum dwellers and complained of being pushed a hundred years back in European civilization. It seems that despite all the miseries it inflicted, the administration demanded love for Stalin and Communism from their victims.

Later it was clear to everyone that the two girls, Helen Doleris and Ona Buzys, were employed by the secret police. When they held their parties it was at the order of the secret police and they wrote down everything that was said. It is hard to understand why these girls consented to be a part of such a dirty business but perhaps the hard life had weakened them morally. The Buzys family had only recently escaped from the horrors of collective-farm life and were now enjoying slightly better living conditions. The same was true of Helen Doleris. There had already been suspicions about the Doleris family because they had such a large section of the jurta compared to everyone else. It was said that such secret police employees were paid at least one hundred rubles extra a month.

The police car took me to the NKVD (secret police) building. That whole day I was processed through various rooms. Later they put me in the basement where I was undressed and very carefully searched. Next all the buttons were cut from my clothing, my shoelaces were removed, all the elastic was taken from my clothing, and I was led to a prison cell and locked in. All this time I was so overwhelmed, so shocked and numb, that I was completely stony-faced. Now in the cell I let go and started to cry and scream. The guard came and told me that loud noises were not permitted.

The cell had one small window, space for four beds and the one big open container for toilet facilities which is so popular in Russia and is called a "paracha." At first I was too upset to notice whether or not the beds were occupied, but after a few minutes a young girl came back to the cell. She was a Lithuanian named Vilkauskas. She began to question me, I talked to her, and it was a good tranquilizer for me. A few minutes later two other women arrived. One was a Polish girl, the other was a Ukrainian woman.

Aldona Vilkauskas was the daughter of a farmer who had been deported with his family from a collective farm. She later was sentenced to seven years because she had copied in her notebook a Lithuanian song about the fatherland and about the deportation, which a Lithuanian boy had given her.

The Polish girl had worked on a collective farm. She was deported from the eastern Polish provinces. One day she was raking hay with some Russian girls when a quarrel started among them. She told them to wait a while, it would be a holiday "in my yard too." This is a Russian expression which means that one day she would dominate *them*. She was reported to the police, arrested, and later sentenced to ten years.

The older woman was from the Carpathian Mountains. She had tried to run away from the deportation camp, was caught and sentenced to ten years. The Ukrainian woman had six children and had no idea where they were or what had happened to them, but I later met her daughter who was also in prison. Exchanging experiences and life stories with this woman helped to quiet me down even more.

Our cell and our beds were clean but the food was poor. The others complained about it constantly but I didn't care. In fact, I couldn't eat at all for the first three days. The regime was very hard. Everything was planned to prevent the inmates from committing suicide and thus preventing the completion of the investigation. A small electric bulb burned day and night. We were not allowed to sleep on our stomachs or to put the blankets over our heads. No loud noises were permitted. Twice a week a thorough search was made of the cell and we were let out, undressed, and searched. We had the privilege of walking outside for thirty minutes every day. The place where we walked was surrounded by a high fence and all windows opening on it were covered. We were not allowed to stop walking and were not permitted to pick up anything from the ground.

Every effort was made to prevent news from traveling through the prison. All during our daily walk or while passing through the corridors or during the investigation periods, our hands had to be kept behind our backs. If two prisoners met in the corridor, one had to stop and turn to the wall and cover her face with her hands. The other had to turn her face in the opposite direction as she passed.

The third night I was called to the investigation room. All investigations in Russian prisons are carried on only at night. No one is permitted to sleep during the day and experience had shown that prisoners weakened by lack of sleep have less will to resist. Some believed that the investigators preferred to work at night because they were paid a double rate.

My first investigator was a young Russian, dark haired and of medium complexion. He cursed a lot but didn't try to beat me. The first night he kept me four hours. It took him a long time to take all the information about me. He asked me about my life in the United States, what work my husband did before he lived in Lithuania, what he was doing now. I saw many American air-mail letters as he leafed through my file. He knew a great deal about me, about my relatives, about my visit to Moscow, and other matters. At first he told me that I could get ten years for my crimes but that he was expecting more material from Lithuania. He investigated me each night during the first week.

The following week another investigator took over. His name was Tibukajev. He was also Russian, young, short, dark haired. He was a quieter type. At first he asked me, "How shall we talk, as friends or as enemies?"

I answered him, "As enemies. If you were my friend you would release me and not keep me here for nothing."

I decided to tell only the truth and to sign anything they asked for. I had heard many times from my cellmates, and even before, that it makes no difference how you behave in prison. Some prisoners cried, kissed the hands of the investigators, promised everything, but still they were sentenced to twenty-five years. Others were very heroic and refused to sign anything which wasn't true, suffered greatly, were tortured, and the result was the same.

He first read the accusation against me—agitation against the U.S.S.R. He accused me of saying that in Irkutsk it was impossible to get any food except fat. I said that this was not true; if I had said anything it would have been that fat was not available; actually, it wasn't possible to buy even margarine. He said that I had expressed the opinions that potatoes wouldn't grow well in Siberia and that American materials were better than Russian; he said he was even afraid to repeat some of my remarks. Supposedly I once said, while eating American canned meat, that in Russia such good meat was eaten only by Stalin. I was accused of saying, while looking at a picture of American cruelties in North Korea, that when the Americans came they would do even worse things to the Communists. There were many anti-American posters at that particular time. Really, I don't recall ever making such comments to anyone.

He spent every night for a week trying to make me confess to being an American espionage agent. He asked what spy mission I had been given by the Americans when I visited the consulate. My reply to that was, "What kind of spy work could I do in the middle of the Siberian forest?"

He said that sometimes a spy waited years before being able to complete his mission. He asked also what secret code I used in writing letters to my husband.

A few times I asked my questioner to tell me something about my son and what was happening to him. His answer was always, "Admit how you spy for America and I will tell you everything about your son."

A few days after the investigation started, Aldona Vilkauskas left for trial. A few days later the Polish girl left and the next day the Ukrainian woman was taken away too. After trial prisoners were never brought back to the same cell. I couldn't bear to be alone and could not help crying but I was alone only a half day when—what happiness!—Two women were led in, Stase Valeckas from our jurta and another Lithuanian, Zose Labanauskas. I was very happy to see Stase. So many things had happened during these three weeks in prison and we had much to talk about.

Mrs. Labanauskas, a middle-aged woman, was in the prison with her husband. They had been deported to a collective farm and both were arrested on the same day but at different places. They left a thirteen-year-old daughter without anyone to care for her. The police station of the collective farm was only a few steps from the barracks in which they lived. She saw her husband in another truck, they both saw their daughter in the yard and she saw her parents, but they couldn't speak to each other or say good-bye. There were four Lithuanians arrested at this collective farm for singing a popular old song which had no political meaning: "Let us go home to our fatherland, let us go home."

The life on their collective farm was hard too. They didn't have sufficient fodder for their cows and were forced to put them out to pasture in the middle of February. The investigators accused Mrs. Labanauskas of trying to sabotage the cows by feeding them crushed glass. It seemed that they were looking for an excuse for the sudden death of the cows on this farm.

I was with Mrs. Labanauskas for about a month. She was sentenced to ten years. Stase Valeckas stayed in the cell for about a month after that.

One night when Stase came from the investigation she said that she had been confronted with Helen Doleris as a witness and Helen told her that Johnny was staying with their family. This was a terrible blow to me, for more than anything else I wanted him to grow up in the proper moral surroundings. I already had written three times to my investigator petitioning to have my son sent to a children's detention home since he had no relatives to look after him.

The weather was cold now but I was still wearing the summer dress in which I had been arrested, and the same underwear. I wrote another petition, as did everyone else arrested from the jurtas, asking permission to get additional clothing and winter dresses from home. The petition was granted but we weren't allowed to ask our relatives to bring the things. During the periods of investigation, prisoners are completely isolated from the outside world. No newspapers are allowed, no letters can be received or sent, and no visitors are permitted. The prison administration sent a sentry to the families of the arrested and told them to prepare a parcel of clothing. My poor little boy prepared everything for me. He sent me a pillow, a scarf, a blanket, a little underwear, and a cotton padded jacket. He forgot to send me such important things as my felt shoes. Later he told me how heavy the bundle was when he carried it about four miles through the city. The guard at the prison gate took it and dismissed him.

In the middle of November another investigator took over. His name was Zuev. He was about forty years old, tall, heavy set, getting bald, and with sadistic tendencies. He told me that he would kill me with pleasure if it were allowed. At first he declared that my case was much more serious than it had seemed before and so he took all the information over again. Later I was told that cases which he investigated usually ended in twenty-five-year sentences. At this time in Russia the death penalty was abolished and the maximum sentence was twenty-five years.

He started asking the same questions which I had already answered twice before. He asked a lot about America. He asked me how America compared with Russia. I said that Russia was a hundred years behind what I had seen in America in 1935. He asked how New York compared with Moscow. I told him to visit New York and then we would talk about it again. He asked me about the questionnaires I had filled out at the American consulate in 1945. Did they include questions about roads, bridges, railroad crossings and so on? He spent a great deal of time inquiring about my relatives in Moscow. Before John left we had agreed to use certain codes in our letters rather than saying everything openly. If I said things were good, it meant bad, and we had decided to call the American Consul "uncle." Now in my letters from John they found "uncle in Moscow" mentioned frequently. I told them the truth about this too for I really didn't have any relatives in Moscow and there was no other explanation. Then he started again about my help to the partisans in Lithuania. I was accused of feeding them. I had never admitted this before and didn't now, though he tried very hard to force an admission from me. He even sent me to a "sabatschnik" which literally means "dog house." It was a room so narrow that you couldn't sit down. Uncooperative prisoners were sent there for a few hours to think things over and I was sent there several times.

He repeatedly asked me to admit that I was an American spy and promised not only to take care of my son but to release me if I would confess.

Finally, one by one, various witnesses were brought up to testify against me. On such occasions there were two investigators present.

The first witness was Helen Doleris. She testified that I had had a photograph made in front of the jurta and tried to send it to John to show how badly I was living. She said that I once asked where the Irkutsk airfield was located. She said she had heard rumors that my husband was now working in the American Legation in Moscow, using a different name and operating as an American intelligence officer.

The next witness was Helen's father. He repeated the accusations which I had heard from the investigators—I criticised Russian materials and claimed that such good food as American canned meats were eaten only by Stalin.

I was given no opportunity to answer or discuss these accusations. I didn't know whether to laugh or cry over all this nonsense. If it hadn't been so serious, it would have been ridiculous.

Next came Ona Buzys. She reported that I had asked what they were doing in certain big factories and that my husband wrote to me that very soon everything would be changed and that the Americans were coming. She said that my husband lived very expensively in America and had even bought another house. Here the investigator interrupted her saying, "Don't bother about what she said is good about America, just what she said is wrong about the Soviet Union."

On December 1 another prisoner was put into our cell. She was a young Ukrainian. During the war her husband had been in Germany, then went to Great Britain as an immigrant, and later decided to go back to Russia. Because of his life abroad they were deported to Siberia with their two children. As usual, their living conditions were extremely hard and her husband started drinking heavily and beating her. She made up her mind to go back to the Ukraine, even without a permit, but was captured on the train. At first she was in a good prison with both of her children but later she was sent to our prison, the older son was given to the father, and the younger son was put into a children's detention home. She suffered terribly, worrying constantly about the children. We talked about our common problems and this was a kind of relief for us.

The food didn't improve and we were always hungry. Fortunately, the prison staff dining room was only a few doors from our cell. Some of the guards were good-hearted fellows and often they gave us an extra saucer of soup. These scraps from the administration kitchen were much better than our ordinary food and we, like animals, counted the footsteps in the corridor every evening and waited. Maybe this time our kind guards would give us an extra bit of food.

The long investigation wrecked me completely. During the whole time I was under unbearable tension and desperately tired from lack of sleep. I was so exhausted that I couldn't think clearly and after a few minutes I would fall off my chair. Finally it seemed that my questioning was over and I was left alone for about two weeks but after three months of nightly questioning I couldn't sleep at night.

On December 20 I was called to the prison office in the daytime and here the Act of Accusation was read to me officially. I was told that my case had been sent to the war tribunal and asked if I wished to have an attorney. I said I didn't; there was nothing an attorney could do to help me.

The next night I was called by my investigator again and told that I had a message from my husband. I didn't know how to react to this and then he added that I had received a parcel from America and would I like to have it?

"Will you give me the parcel?" I asked.

"Maybe," was all he said and I was dismissed.

The next night I was called again, this time to another room. A few investigators and even the prison commandant were present. All were standing around my parcel. While I was on hand as the owner they opened the package and told me that I could not take the things but to sort them out and remove each item from its wrappings. After looking longingly at everything, I asked if I might have a box of dried milk and a scarf. The investigator said I could have nothing, it was against the rules, and that they would send the parcel to my son. I asked them not to send it to Johnny because I knew that the Dolerises would take everything and he would never see any of it. I was asked to sign the receipt as the receiver of the parcel and then dismissed. Back in the cell I scolded myself for signing for the parcel. I was sure now that it would disappear.

Christmas came. I sang with Stase our Lithuanian Christmas carols. We found some carols which were familiar to our Ukrainian cellmate and we all sang together a little. This had to be done in whispers. The religious songs and ceremonies helped the hopeless people so much. Maybe that is why the Soviet slave labor camps and prison administrations oppose religious holidays. The Lithuanian farmers are very devout and it was painful to see how they suffered without any religious help, especially those who were seriously ill or injured. I hadn't attended a religious service, entered a church, or seen a priest since my deportation.

9

The Trial

THE SECOND DAY after Christmas, December
27, at six in the morning I was taken away to a court session. First, as usual, I was thoroughly searched. Later four
soldiers with loaded guns, two in front and two behind, took
me across the street to a court building. Some people walking in the street looked at me and I felt they were thinking
of me as the worst criminal in the world. The soldiers led
me into a waiting room before the court session started.
Two soldiers remained standing guard at the door. I was
alone under terrible mental tension for nearly two hours
before I was led into the courtroom. I felt like telling the
soldiers to go ahead and shoot me.

The courtroom was not very large. There was a big desk
at which were sitting the secretary of the court, the judge,
who was a gray-haired major in the Soviet Army, two
officers who were members of the court, and one more who
was the prosecuting attorney. Near the desk sat a thin, very
old man with a gray goatee; he turned out to be my attorney. Despite my refusal, an attorney had been appointed.
Later I found that I had to pay 250 rubles for his services

and this money was taken from my earnings in the prison labor camp.

I was ordered to sit on a chair opposite and facing the judge's desk. Two soldiers stood by my side and one behind me. A Lithuanian translator was present but I didn't use him much because while working in the children's home for two years I had learned to speak Russian.

After the usual personal questions, they started questioning the witnesses. Now again came Helen Doleris, Ona Buzys, Marinskas' daughter, and the woman with whom I had shared the one-partition jurta. Each of them repeated everything exactly as they had told it before.

The woman from my jurta compartment was very much afraid, pale and shaking. She couldn't speak Russian and testified only in Lithuanian. She reported that I had said that American materials are better than Russian. When an opportunity came, I asked her in Lithuanian where my son was and before the court could stop her, she told me he was still with the Doleris family but that they had been moved away from the jurta.

Mr. Doleris did not appear. Later I learned that some time during this time he had suddenly died. Ona Buzys' mother had died, too, after having a nervous breakdown the day we were arrested. I always have believed she knew that her daughter was cooperating with the Russian police and our arrests were too much for her.

There was no cross-examination. After hearing all the witnesses I decided to behave as usual. The witnesses were called one at a time and dismissed after they had testified. When all the testimony was in the judge asked me why I disliked the U.S.S.R. I told him that I had been deported and had to leave everything behind, now I was forced to work hard but not paid enough to buy bread. Why should I like the Soviet Union?

"But you live so well here," he told me, "because you had so much support from your husband."

"For this support I am grateful, not to the Soviet Union, but rather to America where my husband earns enough money for himself and even enough to support me too."

After this he asked why my husband wrote for me to wait and not lose patience for there would come a time when things would change? What did he refer to when he wrote to me in this way? They suspected that John thought the United States was going to try to change Russia. What could I say to him? Poor John had only been trying to keep my spirits up.

The court recessed for a few hours and then began again. I was accused of being rich, of keeping servants, and of being bourgeois. I said this was not true, that my entire family had always worked hard, my husband was a simple worker in America, and that I had worked in a factory when I lived there.

The court didn't accuse me of spying. Apparently even my investigators found their accusations on this point too vague to press. They asked me again about supporting the partisans in Lithuania, and I again denied it.

Now my attorney made a short speech. In a few sentences he said that his client had been accused of various things against the Soviet Union and that even the name of our great leader was involved.

"But we are not bums," he continued, "we know our

value. Therefore, I don't think it worth while to take the words of Citizen Barbara Armonas too seriously."

Now the court again recessed. The prosecuting attorney held a secret session with the court where I couldn't hear what was said.

About six in the evening the court came back. I was ordered to stand while my sentence was read. According to paragraphs 58, chapter 1A, and 10, I was sentenced to twenty-five years of "corrective" labor in prison and all of my goods were to be confiscated.

There are various degrees of imprisonment in Soviet Russia. I knew of the isolation sentence under which the prisoner spent his entire time in an isolated cell. There are hard-labor prisons, where the inmates work during the day but at night are locked in their cells and must always wear a number. Corrective labor sentences are milder. The inmates are free to move in their dormitories and prison yards after the day's work is over.

I was given a chance to speak my last word. I asked only that my child be taken from the barracks where he was living without proper care and be sent to a children's detention home.

To my surprise I was led back to the same cell after the court session. After telling my frightened cellmates my sentence, I collapsed. I knew now that my life was over and finished, that sooner or later I would die in a prison gang, that I would never see my boy again, nor my husband and daughter. If I could have managed it, I would have committed suicide during those critical hours.

I stayed in the same cell for another week. The first night I couldn't sleep at all. In the morning the prison clerk came and asked me if I wished to make an appeal. I had a twenty-four-hour deadline. The clerk was quite surprised when I said that I didn't wish to appeal. I had had enough of this comedy. I also knew from other prisoners that an appeal only reaffirmed the decision of the court and that life in the isolated investigation prison is much harder than work in the prison gangs.

10

The Transient Prison

AT THE END OF THE WEEK I was transferred to a transient prison located in another part of Irkutsk. Specially built trucks without windows, and with tiny compartments so small that there was no room to move, were used for the transport of prisoners. The Russian population called these trucks "black crows."

In the yard of the transient prison I met the commandant of the investigation prison, who had, I suppose, come there on some business. He smiled at me and said that my American parcel would be delivered to me. I will remember this commandant as one of very few good men I met during my time in prison.

Once in the investigation prison when I was crying very loudly, a guard had reported me to the prison commandant as a noisemaker. The commandant called me in and asked me why I was making such a racket. I had the opportunity then to tell him my story and had seen from his expression that he understood the injustice of my sufferings. Now he was good enough to send my parcel to me, though the decision of the court had been that all my goods would be confiscated.

In the transient prison, the doctor checked me over quickly, then I was pushed into a noisy small cell holding about fifty women. This was an entirely different world. In the investigation prison there had been many restrictions. After the prisoners had been through the investigations and court sessions, no one cared what happened to them. We got our buttons and shoelaces back.

There was a deafening racket in the cell. Women were singing, crying, and fighting. They immediately surrounded me and poured out a barrage of questions: How many years, and what for, were the main points of interest. No one had warned me what to say so I openly said twenty-five years for paragraph 58 and at that they all started accusing me of being a Fascist. Later I found that all the other prisoners were criminals, many of them murderers or members of large bandit gangs, and some who were serving only five, seven, or ten years for minor offenses, but no other political prisoners. There were two Lithuanian deportees serving sentences for stealing food from a collective farm.

The other women were afraid to talk with me because of my crimes but when they discovered my small bundle containing a head scarf and two pairs of American socks they didn't hesitate to take it from me and the articles disappeared.

In a few hours I was called to the prison storeroom. They had sent a few things on from my former prison such as my pillow and a small sack containing about one glass of sugar. The guard told me that there was a parcel there for me. This was my American parcel, which had been opened. When the guard saw what was in it his eyes grew big; he said he had never before seen such things. He was quite a nice person and advised me to leave the contents of the parcel in the storeroom because the other cell inmates would take everything away from me if I took them back there. He found a large suitcase made of heavy boards and with a crude lock. I packed the things into the suitcase, locked it, and took the key with me.

I gave the guard a piece of material as payment for the suitcase, a packet of tea for the lock, and then gave him another piece of material, asking him to sell it for me. I had no money at all and knew I could buy things from the prison store if I could only get a little cash. He promised to sell the material and give me the money when I left the prison.

When I went back to the cell, carrying my sugar and pillow, all the inmates asked where I had been so long. I said that I had to take some things from storage, which they could see, and that I was fingerprinted at the same time. They checked my hands and finding no ink on them hit me in the face, crying, "You lying prostitute, maybe you made complaints about us." I got out of this jam with some difficulty.

I was told that I was now allowed to write a letter and could have a visitor. I had no paper or pencil and couldn't write Russian so one of the women helped me. I wrote to the Stremikis family asking them to give half of the letter to Johnny and to tell him to come to visit me as soon as possible. As Mrs. Stremikis was in prison too, I hoped for sympathy from that family. I wrote a second letter to the prison commandant requesting permission to talk with him. I wanted to try again to have my son admitted to the children's detention home.

That evening we got some cereal. I took a little sugar from my small sack. Another inmate saw me and asked me to give her a little of it. I took my sack and started to shake a few grains in her palm. She became indignant, tore the sack from my hand, and threw it in my face and over the floor.

They even took my pillow away. There were not enough places for everyone to sleep in the bunks, and the criminal aristocracy had all the sleeping space. I had to sleep on the floor, I missed my pillow very much and began to cry. A couple of hours later someone threw my pillow to me.

As usual, there was a leader in the cell. The inmates called her "matka," which means mother. She was a strong middle-aged woman named Lydia, who had been sentenced to twenty-five years for hacking a man to pieces. The criminals called each other "blatnyj"—a word which has no exact translation into English. It means a kind of clever crook.

A few days later a guard came and called out twenty-five names. My heart almost stopped for mine was among them. We were sent to the prison baths and then to the storeroom for our belongings. I was glad to have my big wooden suitcase for no one suspected what was inside. The guard pressed a hundred rubles into my hand, the money he had received for my material. I guarded it carefully and during the night, having covered myself with a blanket, sewed it into the shoulder of my padded jacket. I was looking to black days ahead.

After the baths we were issued additional equipment. I got a dirty sheepskin overcoat for protection against the severe Siberian winter. I had already received felt shoes while I was in the investigation prison because I had only summer slippers when arrested and when the weather got bad I couldn't have gone for the daily walk without them.

Some of our group who were standing in line saw an officer from a camp called Userda which had a bad reputation. The criminal girls somehow knew all about these things. They started crying and dancing around and even tearing their sheepskin coats into pieces. The guards tried to calm them down, but the officers from Userda saw what kind of workers they were getting—hard-core criminals—and refused to take us. After negotiations were completed we were sent back to the cell. I was enormously happy and hoped that this delay would help me to see my son.

Our cell was half empty now, for another group had been taken out, so I was able to sleep in a bunk.

In the cell the traffic was very active. Every day three to five inmates arrived and once a week a transport was sent out to different camps. The officers of various prison camps came there trying to get the work force necessary to fulfill their tasks.

Friday evening a former manager of a children's home, who was sentenced for embezzling, was put into our cell. There were three kinds of prisoners in our prison, political prisoners, criminals, and embezzlers. The embezzlers were of a much better class than the criminals. Hard living conditions made an embezzler out of anyone who had access to the distribution of food and goods, and they were very often caught and sentenced.

The criminals disliked the political prisoners. If I had known that, I would have lied when asked what kind of sentence I had been given. If I had been a murderer or a thief my situation would have been much better.

The embezzler from the children's home was nice. We slept near each other. I told her my whole story and she understood. It gave me relief to know that I had one understanding cellmate among so many toughs.

On Sunday a warden came and started calling names for visitors. I hardly recognized my name, the pronunciation was so distorted, and I couldn't understand when he said I had visitors, a son and a daughter. What could he mean—a daughter? The guard who escorted me to the visitors' room tried to slow me down but I ran ahead, dashed into the room, and saw Johnny sitting with Helen Doleris. I rushed to him and almost cried, he looked so small and pale, but contained myself in order not to disturb him more than was necessary. There were only a few visitors in the room. The guard said that we must speak only Russian. This was difficult for me but I managed somehow. Johnny told me that he was going to school and that he lived with the Doleris family who were very good to him. Helen tried to be kind and sympathetic but I couldn't even look at her. I didn't say anything harsh to her because I knew that would only make life harder for Johnny.

My son asked me, "Mama, what is your sentence?"

I didn't answer him but asked him more questions about his life and his school. But he persisted. I could not bring myself to tell him the truth so I finally said, "Ten years, Johnny."

He exclaimed, "That is good, Mama, most of the others from the jurta got twenty-five years. I will see you when I have finished school and am a big man."

We had only fifteen minutes for our visit and the guard kept urging us to finish. Johnny gave me his new address.

He lived with the Dolerises still but in a much better house in the city. They seemed to have earned a reward for their service to the police. A spy was seldom kept in the same surroundings after trial because they were of no further use to the police after they had been exposed.

When Johnny left the look on my face made the guard ask what my trouble was. I told him my story in a few words, that this was my only son, without relatives, and that my husband was in the United States. He nodded his head and said, "Now I know why you were sentenced." He said that he would not register this visit. I was entitled to only one visit but in this way my son could come again. The guard caught Johnny outside and told him this.

Helen and Johnny had brought me a pound of sugar, a half pound of sausage and a three-pound can of American lard. I took it back to my cell and wasn't concerned when the women divided it. This time they were generous and left me about a quarter of everything. Our "high society" immediately put it all on the table and ate it. That evening I secretly ate the remainder, under cover of the blanket. If they had remembered that I had anything left, another division would have been made.

On the following Tuesday, a very pale woman was brought in. The inmates attacked her as they had me, asking what paragraph and how many years. She just stood there, not knowing what to say. I recognized her as Mrs. Labanauskas with whom I had spent over a month in the investigation prison. We fell into each other's arms as old, good friends. She had been sent from a so-called "white" prison in Irkutsk, one which kept prisoners but did not require them to work. She told me about the living conditions there, which were better than in the investigation prison. She had been kept with one criminal and a young Estonian girl who had been sentenced to twenty-five years, and whose father and mother were also in prison. The mother became insane during the investigation and was sent to a mental hospital, but eventually was cured; I met her later in a labor camp. From the criminal inmate Mrs. Labanauskas had learned many terrible things about camp life and told me to be careful and to be prepared.

I was kept in the transient prison for another week. On Sunday, Johnny came alone. There were many prisoners in the reception room so we could sit close together in a corner and speak Lithuanian. He told me the story about the two thousand rubles in his coat. He was so pleased that the Dolerises were concerned about him that he immediately told them about the hidden money in his coat. They took the money away from him, but since he didn't mention the money in his shoes, he was able to keep that for himself. I reluctantly told him the truth about the Doleris family, pointing out that he couldn't trust them since they were personally responsible for what had happened to me.

He told me that he hoped I wouldn't be sent to Camp 85. He had a friend in school, a Mongolian, whose mother was there and it was very bad.

I asked him to be a good student and to write as often as he could. I knew now that I might never see him again and our parting was heartbreaking. I felt myself beginning to cry so I pushed him out and left the reception room, afraid to look back.

The next week I was still in the transient prison and for

the first time saw Russian political prisoners. There were three of them, two were wives of Russian pilots stationed in Manchuria and one was a Manchurian Chinese woman doctor. The pilots' wives told me that their husbands, accused of spying for America, had been given twenty-five-year sentences. The wives got ten years because they failed to inform the police that their husbands were friendly with Americans. The Manchurian doctor was a friend of theirs and was sentenced for that. They were all educated women, rich, and had very good pillows and blankets. They allowed me to sleep with them in almost luxurious comfort. The Chinese woman had been kept alone in a cell for a whole year. These women believed that only a war could save them but were also convinced that if the war came near to the prison or camp everyone would be murdered.

The next day a transport of ten girls, all criminals, came from another camp. They had jam and white bread with them. Our girls tried to divide this in the usual manner but they were repulsed by the new inmates. I was afraid there would be a real riot in the cell but our criminal girls retired. During the night they stole a good pair of shoes from one of the new girls. When she couldn't find her shoes, she went to the guard and complained. She wasn't sent back to our cell because it was highly probable that she would be murdered as a squealer. Our matka ordered that the shoes be tied on a string and hung out the window, and threatened that any of the rest of us who told where they were would leave this world. Later there was a general search of the cell and we were each searched individually. The shoes weren't found but later another search group came, went directly to the window and got the shoes. It seemed that someone had squealed after all. Three women who were suspected of the theft were sent to the block-house for three days as punishment.

11

Camp No. 104

On February 28, 1952, another transport was scheduled, again selected from the worst criminals, and I was included. It seemed that the transports were arranged according to the number of years of the sentence. Mrs. Labanauskas and I were unhappy about being separated. She tried to talk the guards into arranging to be sent with me but was rejected. I went through the same procedure as before, took my belongings from the storeroom, and was put with the rest into another "black crow."

We didn't know where we were going but my companions tried to guess by the changes of direction. The windowless "black crows" had almost no ventilation and for lack of fresh air some of the women got sick. I kept on crying because I didn't know how far they would take us or if I would ever see my son again. The criminals cursed me, calling me imprintable names; they thought I was crying because I disliked their company.

After about twenty minutes our "black crow" stopped. The women were delighted because they guessed immediately that we were at Camp 104 which was located in the suburbs of Irkutsk. This was supposed to be one of the best camps in the entire region; the work was easy, consisting of tailoring shops and a plant for processing mica, and the camp was known for its liberality. Most of the inmates were short-term criminals and embezzlers, about a thousand men and four hundred women whose living quarters were separated by a high fence.

The camp consisted of a few old run-down one-story houses, each with a few rooms which had been converted into dormitories with two rows of bunks. In each room, called a section, about forty inmates were housed.

I was put into the "third section," a very large room in which 140 women lived. My first impression was not at all pleasant. The room was shabby, dirty, and noisy. We arrived after working hours and women were sitting on every bed. Some were old, some had the appearance of mental cases, and some were talking loudly and noisily. I was left there alone, not knowing what to do, and no one paid any attention to me. In a short time I was approached by an old gray-haired woman named Mary Ruzevuckaja. She was a midwife, Polish by birth, but she had been deported from Lithuania. Another woman, Ona Aviza, from Lithuania, also talked to me. They let me sit on their bed for I didn't have one of my own. Immediately we started telling each other our stories.

Mrs. Ruzevuckaja told me that she had been deported from Vilnius with her daughter in 1941. Her husband, a Polish officer, and son now lived in Poland. They had been living on a collective farm and both the women were arrested there. Mary was accused of saying that life in Siberia was very hard and criticising the Soviet government for its inhuman treatment of people, for which she was sentenced to ten years.

Her daughter was arrested later. During the house search the police found her diary in which she had kept a complete description of their hard life, of their hunger while on the collective farm, and of the inhuman deportations. For keeping this diary she was sentenced to ten years; Mary didn't know where she was.

Mrs. Aviza, a farmer, had been living with two children on a collective farm. Her husband was serving a ten-year sentence in Lithuania. While winnowing grain she had stolen about fifty pounds. Her supervisor caught her and she was sentenced to five years. As a minor offender, she had a good job in the kitchen and sometimes brought us nice gifts such as an onion or a turnip.

In Camp 104 there were two departments in the tailor shop, one for custom work and the other for mass production. I had worked in a tailor shop in America so I was put to work on a sewing machine in the mass-production department. During the first lunch intermission I met people from the custom shop, who were all specialists and mostly political prisoners. One of the best tailors was a Lithuanian named Pakalnis. I met another Lithuanian there whose first name was Paulina, who had been born in Russia and had lived her whole life in Leningrad but could still speak, read and write Lithuanian fluently. I lived with her almost all of my time in prison and her friendship and wisdom were of the greatest help to me.

She was a bookkeeper and had been sentenced for embezzling. Her husband had been killed in the Finnish-Russian war. She herself had been badly wounded at

Leningrad and could hardly move her right arm but, since she was an excellent artist, she was used as a designer in the shop. There were about ten other political prisoners, Estonians, Germans, and even a few Russians. Through the influence of these people I was transferred to them as a helper, but since I couldn't handle an independent job, I didn't expect to remain there long.

Being on good terms with these tailors helped me to sell some of the goods from my American parcel. For my small tea bags I got twenty rubles each and I sold dress material to a woman doctor in the camp. There was competition for this material between a supervisor of the camp store and the woman doctor. When I asked Mr. Pakalnis what I should do, he advised me to sell to the doctor. As a result, the supervisor, a woman, tattled to the political supervisor of the prison. It was a crime for a civil employee such as the doctor to have any business dealings with an inmate. The supervisor called me in and asked if I knew the doctor, but as the doctor was wise in the ways of camp life she had purchased the material through a middleman so I didn't admit that I had sold it to her. Later she was grateful to me for this.

After a short time I was transferred from Section Three to a better one where only forty women were herded together. The highest social class of our room again were the criminals. They didn't want me even to sit at the small table in the room. It was a long time before I was privileged to go into the small cabinet which was assigned to the women. But even so, these women were not as bad as the ones I had arrived with. That entire group refused to work. They were sent to the blockhouse and punished in other ways but they still wouldn't give in and were finally sent away.

I was afraid that the criminals would steal my few belongings so I always carried a small bundle with me. The criminal girls always said, "Look, she is going to the railroad station." The remainder of the parcel I kept in the prison storeroom.

I was surprised at the good organization and comparative freedom in this camp. At six each morning a soldier came into our room shouting that we must get up. From six-thirty to seven-thirty breakfast was ready in our cafeteria, and we worked from eight until noon, had a one-hour lunch intermission, and worked again from one to five. After five our evening meal was ready and then we were free to do as we pleased until ten. We could go into the yard or from one section to another. There was a radio in each room which played until at least eleven every night. We had a big library with books and newspapers but it was almost always empty. Once a week there was a free movie.

The food was bad but almost enough in quantity to keep us alive. We had cereal boiled in water without sugar or fat for the morning meal. Lunch was soup with fish or animal lungs and a few potatoes. In the evening it was cereal again. The bread ration was never sufficient. We could always have eaten twice as much as we received. Sometimes we were given herring or smoked fish of poor quality, which had been rejected for sale in the public stores.

In the men's zone there was a store which had various things for sale such as sugar, jam, bread, and sometimes sausage. A wagon from this store visited our section regu-

larly. We were allowed to receive money orders from outside and the workers were paid a premium if they exceeded
their norms; some of the tailors made thirty to forty rubles
a month. Good tailors such as Mr. Pakalnis and Mrs.
Makus got private orders from the prison administrators
and their friends, filled the orders after work hours, and
were paid extra in money and other products.

Mrs. Makus had owned a fashion shop in the Estonian
capital of Talinn. She had been in prison since 1941, with
her husband who had died here three years before. Mr.
Pakalnis had been arrested at the collective camp to which
he had been deported. His wife and two children remained
there. He managed to send his family about a hundred
rubles each month.

This place was called a re-education camp and we were
considered not as prisoners, but as being "temporarily isolated." The prison was surrounded by a double, high,
barbed-wire fence. Between the fences was a "death zone"
which was raked frequently so that footsteps could be easily
seen. Russians apply this method both to their prisons and
as a means of guarding their borders. Though the criminal
prisoners sometimes attempted to run away, the political
prisoners didn't even try; we had no place to go.

The fence between the men's and women's sections was
not heavily guarded and in the darkness not only men, but
women too, frequently tried to jump the wall. This was not
allowed, but they were not punished very severely; only by
one or two days in the blockhouse. Many criminal women
tried to get pregnant because criminals and embezzlers who
became mothers often were given amnesties. In Russia
amnesties were frequently given to criminal prisoners, but

from the beginning of the Soviet Union up to the time I am describing, there had been no amnesty for political prisoners.

Compared with Novostroika, and life in the investigation prison, the discipline was ridiculously soft. We were not allowed to smuggle letters to visitors, all were supposed to go through the prison control, but everyone tried to get them to the outside through the visitors or through men's teams working outside the prison wall. Anyone who was caught lost the privilege of writing letters and receiving visitors for a period of time. A similar offense committed by a "free" deportee would have resulted in a sentence of ten to fifteen years in prison.

We were permitted to write two letters a month, have one visitor a month, receive as many letters as arrived, and a moderate number of parcels. We had a good bathhouse and were even given a little bit of soap. There was a decent hospital run by inmate doctors but fortunately I enjoyed good health all the time I was there and never was in the hospital. We had a poster-newspaper, art and theater groups, and orchestras. A few times a year the men's orchestra played in the women's section and the women could dance with each other. There was no comparison between the living conditions here and in Novostroika or on a collective farm. It seemed that Communism functioned better for prisoners than for the "semi-free" people. Still, I would have chosen at any time the most miserable period in Novostroika with its comparative freedom to the better-organized life in Camp 104.

Our lives were filled with propaganda. Communist agitators came from the outside world and the cultural leader of our prison forced all prisoners to attend the meetings. We all disliked going, except the gang leaders and prisoners with good jobs who thought that indifference might endanger their situation. We had lectures on the international situation and lots of anti-American propaganda. We heard all these things over the radio, too. Everyone disliked the radio because ninety per cent of what we heard was about increased output quotas and constant thanks to Stalin who gave the workers conditions under which to achieve these quotas.

There were so many internal spies in the prison that it was never safe to show any dissatisfaction or to criticize anything. The head of the tailor shop, a Russian political prisoner, had been sentenced to ten years. Once he was careless and made a critical remark which was overheard by a spy; his sentence was increased by four years.

We were incessantly under pressure to buy government bonds. Prisoners making ten to fifteen rubles a month had to buy a government bond with half of their earnings. Mr. Pakalnis was requested to make a bond commitment but he lost patience and said, "There are enough prison camps in Russia. I will not donate money so that new camps, even for my children, can be built." After this he was frightened, and everyone around him was too, expecting that something awful would happen to him but nothing did. Perhaps as a good tailor he was so valuable that the people in charge didn't want to lose his services.

To our surprise the head of the tailor shop subscribed nine hundred rubles a month for bonds. We couldn't imagine where he got so much money unless someone on the outside was helping him in order to impress the administration and thus get him out. He was praised many times on our wall newspaper and even mentioned on the radio as a great hero because of his sacrifice for the Communist system.

Camp 104 was only six miles from downtown Irkutsk. Visitors could ride the suburban train and walk a mile from the railroad station. I wrote Johnny a letter immediately after my arrival and explained to him how to get there and what formalities he would have to go through in order to see me. A week later I got a sad reply from him. He wrote that the assistant camp commandant had visited the Doleris apartment and taken everything that belonged to us. This was according to the ruling of the court. He even took Johnny's new shoes, claiming that they were too big for him. Not many things remained—all my savings in food and materials had already been cleared out by the Dolerises. My good, durable seal coat which I had brought from America was seized and it was rumored that the assistant commandant's wife was wearing it.

My son didn't come for almost a month. I didn't know why and was very upset. Finally one Sunday the guard called me at seven in the evening saying that a young boy was waiting for me. It was after hours for visitors, but I wanted so much to see him, I begged and cried so hard, that I was permitted to go. He had been waiting for about four hours but, not knowing the proper procedure, he had missed doing something he should have.

He looked very pale and dirty. He brought me a gift of a piece of white bread. He didn't complain about the Doleris family. On the contrary, he said that they were good to him, but I felt he was hiding the facts in order not to

127

worry me. I gave him fifteen rubles to help him out; it was very little, but all I could do.

In April I was transferred back to the mass-production section. The work was hard, the norms were high, and the sewing machines were badly in need of repair. The thread broke constantly because the tension was not properly adjusted so I couldn't make any money by overproduction. From the money I did earn they subtracted a sum for food, lodging, supervision, etc., and I always remained in debt to the government. There was one good thing, though; I was never forced to donate money for bonds.

All the workers around me were criminals and some of them were mean. I remember one especially who sat opposite and always found ways to annoy me. Once I talked back to her and she started to beat me. There was an investigation about this but my experienced friend, Paulina, told me to be as calm as possible because if a criminal was punished because of me, my life would be even more miserable.

Johnny visited me regularly now. In June, he brought his school report card to me. He had finished the fifth grade and his marks were excellent. Out of my meager income from the remnants of the American parcel, I bought some material and made him two shirts and a cap. How to get the things to him was a problem for I was not allowed to take anything to the visitors' room. I put the cap under my babushka, used the shirts for "falsies" and succeeded in passing all three over to him.

Now I didn't try to write to my husband at all. I did write some letters to my sisters in Lithuania but apparently at this time letters from Lithuania and Russia were not being delivered to the United States.

At about this time new political prisoners arrived. One was Lidia Raud, an Estonian woman who had become insane during the investigation and with whose daughter Mrs. Labanauskas had been kept in the investigation prison. After her release from the hospital she was sentenced to twenty-five years. She was so happy to hear about her daughter that we became good friends.

Two weeks later a Ukrainian woman arrived whose name was Efremova, the wife of an officer stationed in Irkutsk. After V Day, while she and her husband were living in East Germany, she praised the German standard of living and said that the Russians were far behind. One of her friends reported this to the secret police and she was arrested. During the investigation the police found that she had worked as a schoolteacher in the Ukraine during the German occupation and this was another big crime, enough for a twenty-five-year sentence. Her husband, trying to save his career, promptly divorced her and even refused to care for their daughter, who was about eleven. The daughter was sent to some relatives in the Ukraine and her husband had been transferred to another unit away from Irkutsk. She received many parcels from some unknown friend and we suspected that her husband was trying secretly to help her.

We even had one Russian student. She belonged to the student anti-Communist circle and had been caught distributing their leaflets. Surprisingly, she got only ten years. I never met Latvian deportees or prisoners. They must have been sent to a different region of Siberia.

At the end of June Johnny visited me again. His clothing was very shabby and he looked thin and hungry. I gave him fifty rubles from my last reserve and told him to go somewhere and get a good meal. When he went to sleep that night, Helen Doleris took forty rubles out of his pocket, leaving him only ten.

The next month Johnny neither came nor wrote. He didn't appear again all summer. I was frantic with worry. I wrote letters to him and even to the Doleris family but got no reply. I shared my concern with everyone and at last on August 30 the guard came to me and said, "Now finally your son has come." I was so excited that I ran to the reception room forgetting even to hide some small things which I had for him, and somehow the guard forgot to search me.

My boy was absolutely in rags. His pants were full of holes. I had no money with which to help him. I had used the money I got for the goods from the parcel to buy additional food in order to survive. I demanded to know why he hadn't written or come to see me and he told me the following story:

Helen Doleris disliked the influence I had over my boy and went to the camp commandant, telling him that Johnny was leaving the city without a permit. A deportee had no right to do this. The assistant commandant talked to him and frightened him by saying he would be sent to the children's correction home unless he stopped these unauthorized visits to our camp. Doleris' son worked on a ship on the Angara River as a boiler operator. He liked Johnny and took him on the boat for about six weeks, with the consent of the camp commandant. Living conditions on the ship were not too bad, he said, in spite of the condition of his clothing.

After he left I wrote letters to my relatives in Lithuania and to friends in Novostroika, asking them to help him and particularly to send clothing. I must have written a good letter, for everyone responded. My friends in Novostroika even took up a collection for him. Due to my arrest and harsh sentence, they were afraid to send the things in the name of Armonas so they sent a gift parcel and new shoes to the Doleris family. Four years later, when I met some people from Novostroika, I learned about the parcel and shoes which Johnny never saw. The Doleris family gave him some things out of the parcels from my relatives in Lithuania, but they took part of those too.

The next month he came well dressed. Organizing all my last resources, I had scraped together forty-five rubles and gave them to him. My son told me about the parcels from Lithuania but begged me not to write anything to the Dolerises about them because it would only make his life harder. I even forced myself to write them a letter of thanks.

I started action again to get Johnny placed in a detention home. One inmate, a Jewish woman sentenced for embezzling, had three children in the detention home and told me the proper channels to use. But my son, under the influence of the Dolerises, was afraid to go to the home so when the inspector came, Johnny refused to leave. I received a letter stating this fact from the administration of the home and adding that they were dropping the matter because he wanted to stay with the Doleris family.

Then on December 4, a very cold day, my son came again and told me that the next day he would be taken to a children's home. The assistant commandant of the jurta camp was taking care of him now and going through the proper channels. The assistant commandant and Helen Doleris had quarreled and he had decided to take Johnny away. Perhaps the quarrel was over the division of a parcel that my husband sent to us; at this time, many parcels disappeared. When I told the inmates that Johnny was leaving for the children's home, they began telling me frightening tales about such homes and about the criminal gangs that flourished in them. I couldn't help but wonder if I had done the right thing.

Two weeks passed before Johnny came again. He looked much better, dressed in a new dark suit with a red tie, and said he was quite happy. He had been sent to one of the best homes in the area and the assistant camp commandant had helped by withholding certain facts about his background. Now he told me about the hard life he had had with the Doleris family. Sometimes he had nothing to eat, he had to stand in line all day Saturday and Sunday waiting for food, and sleep on a hard bench in the kitchen. After New Year's he visited me regularly each month. I was less worried about him now. He had been transferred to a different school and still was doing very well.

During that winter, work in our tailor shop became scarce and it was decided to liquidate the shop. I was afraid that I would be sent to another camp far away from Johnny, but I was transferred from the tailor shop to the mica-processing section. My job was to separate the mica, which was supposed to allow me to earn a little extra money after I became experienced. The gang leaders were always pressing us to increase our output. One day they declared a "specialist competition" among the gangs and I was asked how much I would promise to increase production in the next month. I lost my patience at this and said that I tried always to do as much as I could and simply refused to participate in such a competition. As punishment I was soon transferred to another job which offered less possibility for premium pay.

On March 1 our radio reported that Stalin was seriously ill. All the political prisoners were pleased. We felt that as things couldn't be worse, a change could only be for the better, but we were afraid to show our feelings. The criminals and embezzlers showed concern, but who could tell how they really felt? On March 4 the radio reported his condition as very serious. Some political prisoners who had been to the hospital brought back the news that our doctors thought he would not recover. On March 5 he died.

After the announcement of his death, the radio played only funeral marches and similar music for a full week. The next day a special meeting was held, with speeches praising Stalin and his lifework of creating such an advanced country as the Soviet Union with such high socialistic achievements.

A few times each year we could buy ice cream from our wagon store. By coincidence March 5 was one of those days. Mary Razevuckaja, two others and myself were eating the ice cream when Mary raised hers in a toast to a better future after Stalin's death. A prisoner working as a spy immediately reported this to the administration. Poor old Mary was scared to death when she was called for investigation by the prison political officer. No one investigated me, but anyway I was no longer afraid. They couldn't give me a longer sentence than I already had—twenty-five years.

One day at the end of March our radio blared out something about an amnesty for prisoners. Everyone ran like mad to hear more. The political prisoners were quickly disappointed—the amnesty would not apply to politicals. All embezzlers convicted of stealing less than fifty thousand rubles were to be released. Criminals sentenced for more than ten years had half of the sentence suspended. Only sentences for murders in connection with robbery and of course political crimes were not affected.

There was a tremendous commotion in the camp. On April 10 the administration started processing and releasing prisoners. A special team came from Irkutsk to hold meetings and explain all angles of this situation to the prisoners.

The following Sunday my son came to see me. He thought this amnesty would affect me and I will never forget the look on his face when I had to explain that I was not so fortunate.

Soon so many women prisoners had left Camp 104 that it was clear the women's section would be closed. The prisoners still there went through another investigation and a physical check-up. All Lithuanian women and other political prisoners were told we were to be sent to Camp Userda. I sent a letter at once by a released prisoner asking my son to come immediately to say good-bye. He got permission unusually quickly from the children's home and from the camp administration. I told him good-bye, admonished him to be a good boy, and tried to quiet him by saying that there were rumors around that we might also be released soon. He was now twelve years old and in the sixth grade.

There were new rumors every day. The prisoners, living

in such a hopeless state, tried to lift their morale by spreading all kinds of stories. Mostly they were optimistic—big changes were on the way, amnesties were going to be broadened to include everyone, better conditions were coming, and so on. Sometimes the rumors were bad, like the one that we were being sent to the far north where living conditions were extremely hard.

I had spent almost a year in Camp 104. It had been a very dull life, one of work, worry, and constant striving to get additional food. The general atmosphere was horrible among so many criminal women, none of whom could be trusted, who were always fighting, cheating, and cursing. On the bright side was the small group of political prisoners and, of course, Johnny. John and Donna were so far away and I heard so little of them that they were fading from my mind; they hardly seemed real any more.

I felt that the so-called educational camps were aimed not at re-education but rather for the utmost output of production at the least possible cost. I was told that some years ago the food had been distributed according to your work output, but under that system anyone who fell behind could never hope to recover, and the life span of prisoners had been extremely short. In my time, a more effective system was used. Everyone got almost enough to eat. If you wanted to get anything extra or of better quality, you must reach a higher output than the prescribed norms which were high to start with. For a prisoner, time has no value, so who cared that a hundred hours of extra effort were required to earn one glass of sugar or a half pound of sausage?

12

Camp Userda

On April 25, 1953, we left Camp 104 for good. I kept thinking that I would no longer be able to see my son regularly. I didn't know if I would ever see him again or what was to happen to me in the future. We left Irkutsk in open trucks. As we went through the city, prisoners who knew Irkutsk better than I showed me where various children's homes were located. When we passed the street where Johnny's home was, I could see it from the corner.

After four hours of travel we came in the evening to Camp Userda #272-11. Userda is about one hundred miles north of Irkutsk and four miles from the small village of the same name. This was the camp about which I had heard so much. Some described it as very good, but the criminal prisoners drank chlorine or cut their veins in attempts to avoid it.

The camp was a large agricultural farm, which needed only strong healthy prisoners who were willing to work. When our trucks stopped in front of the entrance gate, we could see long lines of prisoners guarded by soldiers with rifles and leashed dogs. We were told that they were prisoners returning from work and waiting for the routine search. Everyone was checked every evening to make sure no weapons or other prohibited objects were smuggled into the barracks. The same thing was done each morning to prevent the prisoners from taking prison property outside with them.

But old Mary wept with joy because in one line was her daughter Kristina whom she hadn't seen in over two years.

After a check of prisoners, we were processed. Each person was asked for which paragraph she was sentenced, how many years, and how long a time had already been served.

When the gates were opened we were surprised at what a beautiful place this seemed to be. Through the big inside yard there were two wide roads with canals running alongside them. The gates themselves were beautiful and marked with the inscription, "With just work I will pay my debt to my fatherland." There were trimmed ornamental shrubberies beside the roads and a lovely lawn with pleasant displays of flowers. Later I found that these flower gardens were designed by a Latvian artist prisoner, Ona Ansana. At first sight it seemed that people should not be afraid to live among such beauty. The yard was immense. There was a nice big hospital with some new equipment. A large cafeteria was decorated with pictures by good painters, had good hand-woven draperies and flower pots, and the tables were clean. You could believe that you were in a good hotel. The food was similar to that in the other camps—always not quite enough—but of better quality because most of it was produced by the camp itself.

The camp farm was huge, my guess was about fifty thousand acres. There were over a thousand cows, three thousand sheep, several hundred horses, even coal mines and factories. The farm supplied food to many camps and prisons in the area. The prisoners as usual got only the crumbs; despite the many cows, I never tasted milk or even milk soup in the three years of my life there.

There were big buildings for the women prisoners, about two thousand of us. Each house had four large clean rooms with twenty-five beds in each room, each bed having four sleeping places on it. There were white cloths on the tables and decent bedspreads and pillows. Even the traditional bedbugs were missing.

This was an exhibition camp. Guests from other countries were frequent visitors. No doubt they were impressed by the beauty and cleanliness and by our library, Red Corners, and other advantages. (Red Corners are almost like churches to Communists. Pictures of Marx, Lenin, and Stalin hang there, Communist mottoes are on every wall, and you can get Communist literature to read.)

The prisoners, however, experienced difficulty and discomfort in living with all this beauty. We were not allowed to wear shoes in the rooms. We couldn't sit on the beds. Only at ten in the evening after the room orderlies took off all the bedspreads were we allowed to go to bed. No laundry, except for the sheets, was provided. Personal clothing had to be washed in the canals running alongside the road. Even so, we dared not hang our things up to dry because the criminals were always waiting to steal anything available. We tried to dry our clothes behind the beds but they were always damp when we put them on in the morning.

There was also a men's prison in this camp, with about

three hundred inmates. They worked in the fields, on construction, or at mechanical jobs, but the isolation was much more strict and fraternization between men and women was not so easy as in Camp 104.

I met about twenty Lithuanians. They were all from deportee camps, as usual sentenced for small political offenses from ten to twenty-five years. Two of them were young girls, both about fifteen, sentenced to ten years for anti-Communist propaganda. One of them was very bold. When at the end of her trial the judge asked the usual question as to why she hated the Soviet Union, she answered, "I hated it, I hate it now and I will hate it always."

Surprisingly, I met Mrs. Labanauskas and Vera Vilkauskas again, who had been in my cell during the first week of my stay in the investigation prison. Mrs. Labanauskas told me that she, her husband, and two other Lithuanians had had a common trial, held in the district area of their collective farm. She hardly recognized her husband, he was dressed in such impossible rags; the criminal prisoners had forced him to exchange clothing with them.

By selling their piglet and hens, her daughter had collected over three hundred rubles which she gave to the chairman of the collective who was to appear as a witness at the trial. But instead of turning the money over to her parents as she requested and as he had promised, he went on a drinking spree and that was the end of their money.

I never met anyone from the jurtas in Irkutsk who had been arrested at the same time as I. It seemed that I had been wise not to appeal my sentence. All the others had appealed to Moscow and, therefore, remained in the investigation prison a few months longer. In the spring their

sentences were reaffirmed and they were sent with big convoys to remote areas in the far north. At the time of my
transfer in the winter, no convoys were organized for political prisoners so I had been sent with the criminals to a
correction camp close to Irkutsk. This does not mean that
political prisoners ever were separated from criminals. In
the far north they also had criminal prisoners, but there
were fewer of them—and they were the more difficult cases.
Small embezzlers and short-term criminals were not sent
there.

On my second day at Userda I was put into a work gang
with twenty-two other women all sentenced to twenty-five
years in prison. All were Russian and hardened criminals
except for one Lithuanian, Julia Bubenas, a twenty-four-
year-old deportee from a farm. Once she had written a letter from Siberia to her fiancé who was a freedom fighter.
Later he was killed and her letter was found, so she was
sentenced to twenty-five years.

Our team was put to work at changing the soil in cold
frames. We carried the dirt on stretcher-like slabs because
wheelbarrows were not available. It was a hard job. Later
we watered seedlings. We carried water in pails from the
ditch about a hundred yards away, did the watering, and
returned for more. The gardens were extensive and hundreds of women were needed to water them by this antique
method.

When the growing season started, work was even harder.
The doctors' offices were closed for no one had the right to
be released from work due to illness. Everyone tried to
trick the doctors in order to escape work. Schemes to fake
abnormal temperature readings, heartbeats, and rashes were

invented. Some hard-core criminals inflicted injuries on themselves. One favorite trick was to dissolve an indelible pencil in water and wash the eyes with it, which caused a bad inflammation.

Closing of the doctors' offices was cruel for the really sick. On my very first day I saw a mass demonstration, almost a strike. We had been lined up in the camp area for the morning search and when we were ordered to march, one woman fell down, presumably she fainted. It was hard to tell whether it was real or faked, but the guards let the dogs loose to attack her. The dogs started chewing her clothing and there was a tremendous outcry of indignation in the line. Some women jumped in to protect the victim, they were all yelling and cursing the administration and shaking their fists. Immediately more guards appeared and forced the women who were nearest to take the sick woman by the arms and march her on with them.

Our columns, perhaps because so many of us were serving long-term sentences, were guarded very closely. Usually for each twenty-five women there were two or three armed soldiers and one dog which was there to catch us if we tried to run away. In each work area the soldiers put up temporary corner posts and beyond these was a death area; anyone who passed the posts would be shot.

We had been physically weakened by working in the factory dust of Camp 104 so the first days of hard work in the fresh air affected us badly and many of the new arrivals from Camp 104 became sick. I had a high fever and felt miserable. Because I had tried during the first few days to work decently, our gang leader believed me when I complained and allowed me to lie down at the edge of the death zone. A little later, one of the top administration men passed by and kicked me. "What are you supposed to be doing here?" he demanded. Our gang leader explained to him that I really was feeling ill so he allowed me to sit there but forbade me to lie down again.

Each gang had one supervisor appointed from the prisoner group, who was usually a criminal and did no work. If the total output of the gang (a better word for it than team) was good she could remain longer in her preferred position. These leaders tried as hard as they could to push us to higher output.

In the growing season our working hours were from eight in the morning until eight in the evening, and during summer and early autumn we worked seven days a week without holidays. But as seedlings couldn't be transplanted in the hot sun, our work hours were changed. We worked from three until ten in the morning and from five until ten at night. During the midday rest period we couldn't walk around in our nice bedrooms but we were permitted to relax on the floors in the corridors.

Still, the work in the gardens near our barracks was not bad. Later we were sent out to weed the sugar beets and turnips in the big fields which were from three to five miles away. We left our barracks at eight in the morning, walked as slowly as possible to the work area, remained there until eight in the evening and then marched back, reaching home around ten or eleven o'clock. The return trip was not included in our work hours.

The weeding job was very hard, all day under the hot Siberian sun. We were not permitted to take extra clothing with us, so when a rain came we had no protection. Usually it becomes much cooler after a rain in Siberia, so we froze and shivered until the exertion of working dried us off.

The same posts were used in these fields to mark the death zones. To give us a little privacy from the guards, two women would hold up scarves as makeshift toilet facilities.

Lunch was brought to us, as was drinking water, but there were so many teams working that the one horse with a barrel of water couldn't supply us adequately. Many times we were thirsty.

The director of the corrective labor camp was very strict. His name was Dolgopatniuk but everyone called him "the tsar" because he was so haughty. If he met a prisoner in the yard he never paid any attention and wouldn't answer a greeting or question. He lived well. Besides a nice house he had a private car, a motorcycle, and a beautiful white riding horse. He enjoyed a good reputation with the higher administrators because the farm output remained good and the cost low.

I was always hungry. I needed more food for hard outdoor work than we were allowed. My parcels were used up and my money was gone. Here, as in Camp 104, after fulfilling a work norm, certain premiums were paid for extra production but we were almost never able to exceed our garden or weeding norms so I started a side income by making small tobacco pouches from remnants of material, stitching pretty patterns on them with colored thread, which Paulina, who had been appointed a storekeeper, drew for me. I sold the pouches for five to seven rubles each. Other girls envied me this side income; they said, "For you it is better here than in America."

At first Johnny wrote to me regularly but during the summer his letters ceased and I became upset about him again. I wrote twice to the children's home asking what had happened to him and at last, after three months, two letters arrived, one from the director of the home and the other from my son. It seemed that in the spring after school was over there had been a doctor's inspection of all the children. A woman doctor making the inspection was sympathetic to my son and told him he should complain about the pains in his joints so that they would send him to a resort. He was pale and underweight and with the help of this doctor's testimony he was admitted to a resort a few hundred miles east of Irkutsk. He forgot my address which was why he couldn't write me. The director explained the same thing to me in his letter.

I decided to make a photograph album as a gift for Johnny's coming birthday. For covers I used material stitched in a nice pattern. Paulina again made a drawing for me. Many prisoners, seeing what I was doing, asked that I make albums for them, and so I had another source of income. I charged fifteen to twenty rubles for an album, and could make one to one and a half each month. There really was no time available but I managed to steal a half hour each morning and evening. The money enabled me to buy some sugar or fat. Even so I don't think that I could have stayed well if a parcel had not arrived from my relatives in Lithuania. They sent me eight pounds of lard which I put in the storeroom under Paulina's care so it wouldn't be stolen. I used it very sparingly and thus managed to improve my diet.

In the autumn I was transferred to the grain store. The

work was hard but many prisoners liked it because good workers could fulfill their norms and make twenty-five to thirty-five rubles a month extra. There was a four-woman gang used here. One person fed grain into the hopper of a winnower, two turned the wheel, and the last woman pushed the cleaned grain into piles. The norm was nine tons a day. The first day we worked very hard and managed to do about six tons. The same thing happened the next day. That meant no pay. A team of Russian girls working next to us were doing between eleven and twelve tons a day which meant a nice premium. We asked them the secret of how to do so much but they refused to tell us. Later at lunch, however, one of them advised us to open the screen a little so the grain would go through faster, though not so clean, while the girls who turned the wheel should also push uncleaned grain into the cleaned pile with their legs. So we began cheating too. Our greatest worry was that the supervisor might see our method of working, but by being alert we escaped detection and punishment. When we saw a supervisor approaching, we immediately hit the screen into position and stopped our leg maneuvers.

After cleaning the grain we started on grass seed, which was an even easier job. It was impossible to distinguish cleaned from uncleaned seed just by looking at it, so we opened our screens wider. When our supervisor went to breakfast we worked very quickly putting the uncleaned seeds into sacks, and in this way we fulfilled our norm and made good money, too. A year later there was an investigation because the grass seed sold by our farm was of such poor quality.

Then came a hard winter. Our sleeping quarters were

overcrowded and so poorly ventilated that we couldn't rest. It was very cold outdoors and almost as cold in the grain storeroom. Our winnowers raised so much dust that we could hardly see each other. Most of the workers were criminals, and as the supervisor was also a criminal she was always on their side and she tried to put as much work as she could on us.

In the next room were two big ovens which burned all the time to keep the temperature right in the rooms where the grain was being dried. These ovens were used by our criminals for unexpected meals. One day a goose, the private property of the commandant, waddled into our storeroom. It was promptly killed, cleaned and baked. There was an investigation but nothing was found except a few bones and feathers; the culprit was never caught. Some time later a goat wandered into our area. He too was promptly and quickly processed. Soon afterwards, a shabby work-worn woman came looking for her goat. She was one of the few free people who lived in the vicinity of the grain storage rooms, which were outside the camp. She said she had five children and the goat was important to the family. She cursed us and shouted that she hoped we would never be free again. I was sorry for her.

One morning, being preoccupied with my tobacco pouches and albums, I hurried to the line, leaving my small purse lying on our room table. In it I carried some pouches, a few rubles and my spoon. The moment I realized I had left it I ran back but everything was gone. I didn't care, except for the spoon. There was a shortage of spoons and it was impossible to get one from the camp. Finally, after a month I was able to buy a spoon from another prisoner.

In the meantime I ate my cereal with a wooden paddle and drank soup from the bowl. While I was in the transient prison, more experienced prisoners had told me to steal a spoon from there because there were none to be had anywhere else. I did this and broke off half the handle because the name of the prison was stamped on it.

Near Christmas time it was very cold, about sixty below zero. We finished our work in the grain storage and were sent to work in the fields to open underground storage silos. These were holes dug into the ground, filled with beet leaves and other greens, and covered with about six feet of soil. They were located three to four miles from our camp. Our twenty-woman gang had the job of uncovering one silo each day. We worked on the frozen soil with wedges and picks but it was hard work. Even harder was the long walk, knee deep in the snow. Because of the extreme temperatures, even our faces had to be covered with scarves. Careless exposure meant immediate frostbite.

I was troubled very much by toothaches during this time but we had no dentist. A few times a year a dentist came to the camp for a few days. The lines of patients stood after work until midnight so there was almost no chance for relief.

Christmas of 1953 came. In Lithuanian tradition the most important part of this holiday season is a special feast called "kucios" on Christmas Eve. In this feast over ten traditional dishes are served, everything without meat, fat, or milk or milk products. There are various kinds of fish, herring, beet soup with special mushroom sauce, cabbage soup, and special desserts, one of which is boiled whole wheat served with milk, prepared from malted poppy seeds diluted with water. Before the meal, the members of the family who are gathered together exchange "oblats"—white thin cakes similar to those used in the communion service—and Christmas greetings.

We could not have our traditional dishes but some of our young girls had received parcels from relatives, which helped us all. The Lithuanian prisoners sat and prayed and cried together, each thinking about her own family, and I about my son especially whom I might never see again and about my daughter and my husband so far away in a different world.

All during midwinter we worked at opening storage silos. Each evening after work I first went to the storeroom where Paulina worked and asked about letters from Johnny. The answer was always the same: there is no letter. Each day became more difficult for me.

On March 3 when I came from work the news was spread that Paulina was going home. I went to her, we embraced and wept. She was happy that she was leaving this hell but for me it would be even worse for I was losing my best friend and adviser. She knew, much better than I, the Russian customs and prison life.

There were rumors in the prison that the government was no longer praising Stalin so highly. We were very curious to know if this could be and asked Paulina to write us about it. If it was true, she was to write "Grandfather is forgotten," but if nothing had changed she was to say, "Everyone speaks of Grandfather." I asked her to visit the children's home when she got to Irkutsk and write me at once, even if something had happened to my son.

On March 6 the entire Lithuanian population accompanied Paulina to the prison gates. After that, waiting for news from her about Johnny was a nightmare. I could hardly sleep. Ten days later, when I came back from work, I found two letters. One was from Paulina. I had to force myself to open it, I was so afraid.

She said that Johnny was alive and healthy but no longer at the children's home. She had talked with the director of the home, who told her that there had been an army team there selecting musically inclined children to educate for future positions in military bands. They chose thirty children and Johnny was among them. She told the director that his mother was very worried about him, since she had heard nothing for so long. He sat down immediately and wrote me a letter, which was the other one I received that day. Paulina asked for Johnny's new address but the director told her it had been decided that this information should not be given out. He did tell her that he was not far from the capital of the Autonomous Buriat Mongol Republic at Ulan-Ude.

The director, in his letter, said that my son had been taken from the children's home but he couldn't tell me the address. He advised me not to worry, that Johnny was being well cared for and would go to school where he was. He said, "Don't interrupt his career. I can understand your feelings as his mother because I have children myself."

Enclosed with the letter from the director was one from Johnny. It said, "Mother, I am going to a military unit. I will not write to you any more, Mother, it is forbidden to me. How I will live and what I will do you are not supposed to know. So I am told by the supervisors. Maybe we will meet again when I will be grown up. Good-bye."

After reading his letter, I fainted. When I had been revived, some kindhearted women cried with me. My last joy and hope had been taken away. His letters were what I had looked forward to and what I lived for. If I could only have a letter from Johnny I could be happy; the future seemed more hopeful even with the work and hardships. Till now I had always had the desire to live and go on. After this letter, I became so sick I was released from work and stayed in bed for three days. Whenever other women got letters my heartache revived. I did not know whether I would ever find my son again or not.

We were set to preparing manure for the fields. The huge piles of manure were frozen solid and it was hard work breaking it into pieces with our simple tools.

Paulina wrote again, this time from Leningrad, saying that everyone had forgotten grandfather. We were sure of this already because on the anniversary of his death the supervisor of the Red Corner in our camp put a black ribbon on the picture of Stalin and the cultural supervisor ordered it removed. In the evening there was a concert for our camp. A military band from Irkutsk performed gay melodies, in contrast with the extreme air of mourning a year before.

Already rumors were spreading about coming changes, relief in camp life, and amnesties even for political prisoners. In February one definite innovation was announced; a new way of apportioning the time served in prison in relation to the degree of hard work performed. For example, each day of heavy work in the grain storage was counted as three days completed on your term. This was a big lift, especially for those who had only a few years left to serve.

We started again on the seasonal cycle, and we were sent to the grain storeroom to prepare the seed for spring. First the grain was processed through the winnowers, then sent to a power-driven grain-cleaning machine. Our job was to put the cleaned grain into sacks and carry them to trucks. Each sack weighed over a hundred pounds so it was a difficult task. We again cheated as much as we dared in order to get premium pay. Our periods of greatest accomplishment were during the breakfast and lunch breaks for our supervisors, when we jammed everything into sacks as fast as we could.

I received letters from my relatives in Lithuania saying that they had started getting letters from America again. After more than a year I finally received, through Lithuania, some news from my husband. I wrote letters back to Lithuania, not through camp censorship but by smuggling them outside the camp. As in Camp 104, visitors often helped, and sometimes women working without supervision in the camp area and having contact with free workers would pass on our letters. I attempted in the same way to send a letter to John but it never reached him. Some letters from him got through to me and some disappeared.

In one letter my relatives said they had sent me three pictures of my husband and Donna. I was convinced that the camp censor was holding them. Once I met him passing through the camp and asked about my letters and why they hadn't been given to me. I even wrote to the political camp investigator and asked him for a personal audience.

One night he sent for me to ask what the problem was. (In the usual fashion, the investigators and other officials called for the prisoners during the night hours.) I complained about the disappearance of my letters and demanded the pictures. He promised nothing but said he would look into the matter. After a few questions about my relatives in America, he released me.

Not long afterwards, he called me, again in the night, and showed me three pictures. One was of Donna, already a grown-up young woman, leaning on a car. The second showed my daughter and husband near a church. In the third Donna was dressed as a bridesmaid. The investigator, who had never seen a costume like it, told me, "The devil knows what kind of dress this is."

The last pictures I had seen of my daughter had been taken six years before. Then she was a child, now she was grown up, and so good looking with such an open honest expression on her face. Longing to study every detail of the pictures, I asked that they be given to me. The investigator refused, saying that they would be bad for camp morale. I wept and begged but to no avail. Finally he lost patience and shouted, "Forget about your husband and daughter, you will never see them again." I told him that any human being has the right to hope until he dies.

(The events of that night made such an impression on me that when our family was finally reunited and we had a color photograph made of the four of us together, I sent a print to the investigator of Userda Camp in Siberia with a note saying, "See how good it is to hope.")

In the month of July our radio started blaring about the arrest and sentencing of secret police chief Beria. Ordinarily we didn't pay much attention to the political news on the radio because it was never more than a monotonous repetition of Communistic achievements, but Beria's case

amused us immensely. His accusation covered many paragraphs, including all those for which I had been sentenced.
Political prisoners had hoped a long time for the fall of
Beria. We thought that any change in such a high-level
personality in Russia could only be good for us. From that
day on, the criminal prisoners, when cursing us, no longer
called us Fascists. Now we were "Beriaists."

The rumors about amnesties had some substance. On
July 25 our camp was visited by high officials from Irkutsk
who called a meeting of the camp inmates in the cafeteria
and announced that there would be an amnesty for some
prisoners. Embezzlers of more than fifty thousand rubles'
worth of state property and inmates guilty of murder with
robbery were excluded. Political prisoners sentenced for
paragraph 10 were eligible, but those sentenced under 1A
were not, among whom I, of course, was included. The
political prisoners under amnesty were released if they had
served two thirds of their terms and, due to the extra days'
allotment, this affected many. It was the first time any
political prisoners had gained an amnesty and made a deep
impression.

The announcement caused much commotion in the
camp. Some were jubilant, others were crying and cursing.
No one from the Lithuanian group could leave with the
exception of two very young girls who were released because they had been sentenced before they were sixteen.

After a week the first amnestied people started leaving.
With their departure work discipline disappeared. The administration held meetings and swore and threatened, but
it took some time for them to regain control.

Somehow this amnesty changed the basic discipline in

the camp. A few weeks later there was a demonstration, almost a strike, in which the prisoners won their point. One day we came from the fields in a rainstorm; we were completely soaked. The administration sent us to the baths without letting us first go to our rooms. We disliked this for we wanted to be able to exchange our wet clothing for dry things. The long lines of prisoners began to protest by screaming and shouting insults, calling the administration "Tscekists" and Fascists. (A Tscekist was the name of the old secret police during the time of terror after the revolution.) Then we simply refused to move. Neither persuasion nor threats had any effect. After an hour of silent battle the administration gave in and we went to our rooms to pick up dry clothes.

The next day, August 20, someone told me to go to the cultural center as I came from work. She said, "There is a big parcel there for you with postage due of twenty-five rubles." I had only five rubles at the time so I borrowed the money from Julia Bubenas, who always had a little extra.

I didn't know what the parcel was but hoped it was from America. I was afraid to tell anyone of my hope, and I lay awake most of that night. When I came from work the next day the custodian of the cultural center said I was expected immediately in the administration center. When I entered the office I found the assistant camp director, the supervisor of cultural activities, political investigators, and others gathered around the desk. On the desk was a parcel from America sent to my Lithuanian home address and forwarded to Userda. The cultural supervisor said, "So you still have relations with America."

"Russia has relations with America too," I answered.

They asked me to take all the items out of the package. They were mostly materials and used dresses. The men searched each piece, took all the labels and sent them away to be checked for invisible ink, and burned the cardboard box as a possible source of secret messages. I got the labels back from Irkutsk three weeks later.

I pushed everything into a sack and as quietly as possible took it to the main storeroom where the supervisor was Lithuanian. She was so impressed with the parcel that she called me "Mrs.," a term of dignity which I hadn't heard in many years.

The next day I took the things to the storeroom for our barracks. Since the supervisor of this storeroom was a Russian criminal, I gave her material for a skirt to forestall her from making an agreement with other prisoners to steal my wealth.

Soon everyone who was Lithuanian knew of my parcel and begged me to sell them something. I sold the things as secretly as possible and almost immediately acquired a few hundred rubles. Even a Russian, our work gang leader, heard of it and said with envy, "Now you are a rich and happy woman." It is surprising what a high opinion these Russian criminal women living in the heart of Siberia have of the United States. I think that their ideas are almost rosier than reality.

The next day I decided to send a letter directly to John, not through the camp administration, but by smuggling it out to the nearest post office. I recently found it in my husband's file:

Dearest Donna and John,

I thank you as much as I can, dear John, that you haven't forgotten me. Many years have passed since cruel fate separated our family and killed the happiness that we knew with our children. Today it is exactly fourteen years since we were separated. Even today I hear the crying of little Donna—"Dear Mama." I always weep on the anniversary of our separation.

Thank you very much for the parcel. I got everything all right. It was so nice to see Donna's used dresses. How happy we were together. Now Donna is twenty years old and Johnny is fifteen.

Johnny is healthy and a good student but he doesn't live with me any longer. I know that he is a good sportsman and plays in an orchestra. He is now in the fourth class of secondary school. I am alive and healthy and live well.

I was afraid to tell them openly that I was in prison. I knew I would be punished if the censor found that in my letter. I remembered our code agreement: if I were in prison I would write that I was sick, so I continued:

You asked me how Aunt Barbara lives. She is old and three years ago she got sick and was taken to an old people's home because she had no home of her own and her health would never be good again. Her foster son, half-brother of Donna, Johnny, was taken to a children's home. Aunt Barbara is very unhappy about this because she can't live with the child who she loved very much. He was her only joy.

I kiss you both,

Mother and Wife

I later wrote other letters saying that I was sick but my

husband had forgotten the code and for several years didn't guess what had happened to me.

In September I went to work in the grain storage again, and the same cheating and the same troubles followed. After the amnesty, our camp had had a number of vacancies, but new transports of embezzlers and criminals arrived until the camp was filled again.

In October we had more very good news. A new law was announced which allowed all political prisoners to petition for leniency. Everyone applied, including me.

Because of the income from the parcel my life was much easier now, but this time I was more careful. In Novostroika, so many parcels from America had made me a rich woman in comparison with the others; therefore, I was considered a bad example and a tool of American propaganda. Now I understood that was the main reason why I had been sent from Novostroika to Irkutsk where a false case was fabricated against me. I determined not to show any evidence of change. I wore the same rags and continued to be a good worker, as I always had been.

When November came, which was my son's birth month, I couldn't stand being so completely isolated from him any longer, so I started planning some way to gain knowledge of his whereabouts. I asked as many prisoners as I could, and every new arrival, about Buriat Mongol, Ulan-Ude, and the troops stationed there. I learned that there was a very large military base about six miles out of the city.

In December the administration commenced another screening of prisoners. Each person was taken to the office and asked about her sentence. What paragraph, how long she had served, and the present whereabouts of her family.

A few months later political prisoners with long-term sentences were transferred to other camps. Only two of the long-term prisoners remained at Userda, Julia and myself. Julia was a good tailor so I could understand her case, but I never could explain why I was left there. At about the same time, long-term criminal prisoners were also sent away; most were murderers in connection with robbery, and I was surprised that there were over 150 of them. In general, Userda was not a prison for long-term inmates so it was thought that other prisons probably had even greater numbers. Political prisoners, commenting on the fact of so many robbers and murderers among women, thought that perhaps Soviet Russia had the largest percentage of such people in the world. One witty Ukrainian said, "You are all wrong. This is nothing more than the result of equal rights between men and women in the Soviet Union."

After their departure in the early spring, the camp was filled up with new arrivals, all embezzlers and criminals.

Again Christmas came. One of our inmates, Ona Samas, got a parcel from Lithuania containing "oblats," which we divided between us. This year we sat together a little longer than usual singing our Christmas carols in hushed voices.

Winter brought the same hard work in the grain storage and later the opening of silos and manure processing. In February, 1955, our camp was cleared of long-term prisoners and was declared a free-regime camp. Now each gang had only one guard and no dogs or visible guns. The barbed-wire fence around the camp remained but the dogs which had been on runs around the camp disappeared.

Usually Userda's inmates had only a few visitors because

of the long distance from Irkutsk and the poor means of transportation, but now an extra house was built for visitors and the rule was changed from a thirty-minute visiting period to two days. The prisoner still had to go to work as usual but was allowed to spend his free time in the evening and at night with the visitor.

On February 25 I received from the American Embassy an inquiry asking me to confirm my address, describe my living conditions, and give the address of my son. I was afraid to answer without proper advice and went to the camp political investigator for help. He instructed me to give the address of the camp, to say I was working and not living badly but not to mention that I had been arrested or was in prison. I didn't know my son's address so I sent the address of the children's home.

In March, with the help of the work dispatcher, who was friendly because I sewed little gifts for her, I got a job in the camp area which was much easier than being in the field gang. I worked with another inmate in the children's laundry, which had no machines, only a kettle for boiling water. We did over six hundred pieces of laundry by hand each day, mostly diapers and children's dresses.

Many women were pregnant when arrested, and some became pregnant during imprisonment so that we always had about fifty babies in our infants' home. The pregnant women, during the last months, and women with newborn children had certain privileges. The new mothers were not sent to work outside the camp and could leave every two hours to feed their babies. Everyone envied them because they spent most of their time walking back and forth.

The children were kept in the home until they were two

years old. On their second birthday they were sent to a children's home outside; the mothers were not told where they were. It was heartbreaking. The mothers cried and screamed and some even went crazy and were locked in bunkers until they quieted down.

Next came another political event which we enjoyed very much. This was the famous fortieth anniversary of the Communist Party at which Khrushchev publicly denounced Stalin. We heard on the radio of the statement which had been made at this conference that many people in the Soviet Union were unjustly imprisoned. Another ray of hope.

Also, I had some success in the search for my boy. A Russian woman said that her son was in the army at the big base near Ulan-Ude. I asked her to write him to inquire if there were any young orchestra players in his camp. He answered that there were. I gave this woman my son's name and asked her to find out if he was there. It was a great joy when, in about three weeks, I obtained a proper address with the number of Johnny's unit. I wanted to write him but was afraid I might harm his position. I knew the address of one of our young Lithuanian girls who had been released and now lived with her parents in Irkutsk so I prepared a gift parcel, smuggled it out, and sent it to him in her name. Very quickly the girl got a telegram: "Parcel received, signed Simoliunas."

The girl wrote to me but I couldn't understand why the signature was not my son's, and yet was typically Lithuanian. I decided to write to Simoliunas, in the girl's name, asking about Johnny, pretending he was an orphan from Lithuania. According to my letter, the girl had known his

parents and was concerned about his future. When Simoliunas got this letter, he was surprised that my son was Lithuanian. The whole mix-up happened by sheer accident, for
there were only two or three Lithuanians on the entire base.
When he confronted my son and asked about his parents,
Johnny answered that they had died and he knew nothing
of them. It turned out that Simoliunas had sent the receipt
because he was the mailman of the unit.

After this I asked the girl from Irkutsk to invite Johnny
to see her on his vacation if it could be managed.

There was another summer campaign of agricultural
work at Userda. All physically able women were checked
and sent to the hardest jobs. I worked again in the grain
storage, this time on the night shift.

In the middle of summer came the results of our ap-
peals for clemency. Julia Bubenas' sentence was cut from
twenty-five to ten years and nearly everyone was given similar cuts except me. No one told me why I had been excluded.

On August 5, something completely unexpected happened. During the lunch intermission prisoners told me
that the guards were looking for me. When I met them
they said that my son had come to visit. I could hardly believe it, but they said I could see him as soon as certain
formalities had been completed. He had to make an application to stay with me and the signature of the camp commandant must be obtained for approval. This took about
two hours but it seemed like two weeks.

At last I saw Johnny. He looked very thin and I had
thought he would be taller. When we began to talk I was
surprised that he had almost forgotten how to speak Lith-

uanian. I hadn't seen him for over two years and he had been living in an entirely Russian world with no need or opportunity to speak anything else.

The girl in Irkutsk, whose invitation he had accepted, gave him my address and encouraged him to come to see me.

He had ridden to the village of Userda in a truck, had then walked the five miles to the camp, and wasted a lot of time trying to find the proper offices. I ordered good food from our cafeteria for him. It was possible to get quite decent food if you paid a big price.

He was supposed to leave after one day but I asked if the visit might be extended for one more day. We talked a great deal and my questions and interest in his problems warmed him so much that he was immensely happy. He left me promising to write and I received letters twice a month from then on.

From our conversations I knew that things had worked out well for him. He could go to secondary school, whereas ordinarily children's home inmates were sent to work after finishing seven years of schooling. It was a fine opportunity for Johnny, but the military unit wouldn't take children of parents living abroad or of political prisoners, so the secrecy which was so cruel for me was best for him.

After the grain season ended, I was sent as a cleaner to the mica-processing factory similar to the one in Camp 104. Mica is used extensively as insulation in the electrical industry of Russia. I worked from twelve midnight until eight in the morning. The work was hard and unhealthy because mica dust injures the lungs. I wasn't able to finish within the regular hours, so I had to work on week ends.

The cleaning job had to be completed and if I didn't do it
I would be replaced or perhaps punished.

In October Mrs. Labanauskas left as the result of her
appeal for leniency. Her husband was released about the
same time and they went to live with their daughter. They
weren't permitted to return to Lithuania so he got a job on
the railroad and died very soon, after enjoying only a few
months of freedom.

When a good friend leaves prison your emotions are
mixed. You are glad for them and join in their happiness,
but at the same time it is very difficult to accept the fact
that you must remain behind. It was a tremendous relief
when I was called to the office where a letter was read to
me stating that due to good behavior and good work, my
sentence had been cut to ten years. I had already served
almost five years and had accumulated about a year of extra
days. Now I planned to shorten my prison time even more.
I asked my friend the dispatcher if she would put me on
the hardest kind of jobs which counted as two or even
three days for one. In this way I hoped that in two to three
years I could be free again.

During this autumn I received another parcel. There
were, among other sorts of clothing, many head scarves. I
gave them all to my Lithuanian friends but there were not
enough so I wrote to my husband asking for more. I felt
bolder than before but I still handled my parcel very carefully. If I sold anything on the black market, I sold only to
very good friends, reliable people, and secretly, and no one
could tell from any outward appearance that I was a woman
of means. There was not such a big fuss made over the
second parcel and the cardboard box wasn't burned, though

the clerk handling the shipment challenged my right to the parcel saying it would not be good for camp morale. After telling him the story of my first one, I persuaded him to give it to me.

Another amnesty was announced, this time for women seventy years and older. My friends Mary Ruzevuckaja and Maria Ivanovna were released. Maria was from a highly educated Russian family and spoke at least five languages, including fluent English, but was sentenced to ten years because she had worked as an interpreter in Germany, with other Russians sent there during the war. She had no relatives left and didn't know where to go. My friend in Irkutsk was a very ambitious woman and before her release had taken English and French language lessons from Maria. Somehow Maria felt closer to the Lithuanian political prisoners than to her compatriots so she decided to go to Irkutsk and stay with my friend for a while.

It was an entirely different story with Mary. She was with her daughter and disliked leaving the camp, especially since she had no place to go and had no idea whether her husband or son were alive in Poland. After the declaration was read to her and she was told that she would leave in a few hours, she hid herself so well that a full day's search couldn't find her. After the transport had gone, she reappeared. In two weeks the same routine was repeated. The next time the administration was more clever. Mary was told that the transport was ready, she was grabbed, her belongings were packed, and she was whisked away. Somehow this old woman got a job in Irkutsk as a nurse in a home for the insane and came back very often to see her daughter.

Just before Christmas I got two letters, one from my husband with a nice Santa Claus picture and Christmas greetings, and one from my son. The eight Lithuanians remaining at Userda gathered in the tailor shop since Julia had obtained a permit for our meeting. We put a branch of spruce on a table and set the gay picture of Santa Claus on the top. This time our mood was better. Many people had been released, our own sentences had been cut, and we could hope that someday even better things might come.

After Christmas one of the clerks in the administration, a good friend of mine, told me she had been in a meeting of the camp administration and a decision had been made to send me away. They were very much concerned about my packages from America and thought that I was an undesirable person. I told this to our Lithuanian girls in secret and they were afraid for my fate. I was frightened too but nothing happened. There was no transport formed from our camp and generally one prisoner was not sent out alone.

After the New Year I started working in the kitchen. One day of work there counted as two. There were six big boiling kettles for different foods. I cleaned them, cleaned the whole kitchen every day, painting the big stove with whitewash, assisted in the cooking, and brought wood for the fire. The work was especially hard because there was no running water, drains, or sewers in the kitchen so I had to carry all the water in a pail from a big barrel outside and then take the garbage out in pails to a hole a few yards away in the field. The kitchen fed two thousand people each day.

The kitchen cleaners had access to various storerooms so the administration was careful in selecting reliable personnel. There had been occasions when large quantities of food disappeared from the storerooms and were sold to prisoners in the black market. I never took part in the big schemes but could not resist stealing moderately, a pickle or a cup of sauerkraut. I hid these extras in my felt shoes and passed them to my friends outside the kitchen.

The schedule in the kitchen was twenty-four hours of work and then twenty-four hours of rest. Such a stupid arrangement almost killed me. I began to lose weight, felt ill and knew I couldn't take very much more.

My morale was better, however, for after the free camp regime was started I got almost all the letters John sent me and got them straight from the United States. My third parcel also came. I sent parcels to my son and at Christmas time even managed to buy a hen, which I broiled and sent to him as a delicacy. The weather was so cold that the hen reached him frozen solid and in perfect condition.

In February of 1956 I couldn't stand any more kitchen work and, with the help of my friend the work dispatcher, was transferred to the bathhouse. The days were counted double here too but it was much easier than the kitchen. Again there was no running water. Water was supplied in barrels brought by oxcart and we took it in pails up a ladder to a barrel high in the bathhouse. Due to the difficulties of the supply and the thousands of prisoners who used the baths, water was rationed to a small pail per person. The bathhouse was used from six until twelve in the evening and one of my duties was to see that no one used more than her share of water. The others working in the baths were all criminals.

I finally learned how to get along with the criminal prisoners: Never fight with them, pay attention to everything that they say, and try to convince them that you will follow their leadership. After I adjusted my behavior they liked me and when I was leaving the camp and told them good-bye, a few of them cried and asked me to write and even gave me small gifts.

In Novostroika life had improved slowly but in Userda nothing changed and no improvements were made during the three years I spent there. Various simple labor-saving devices, sewage systems, or plumbing would have been a tremendous help, but it seemed no one cared that we put in thousands of hours of unnecessary work.

In March there were rumors again that we were to be sent out. We had already started to collect money for another big traditional holiday, Easter. On March 28 the bathhouse supervisor told me secretly that all political prisoners were to be transferred but asked me not to mention it until evening because she knew everyone would stop work at once. I was helping to repair an oven at the time, carrying bricks in and out. I pretended to be sick, was given time off, and wrote a letter to John sending him this news. In the evening the announcement was officially made. Everyone was much concerned about why we were being sent away and where we were going.

The next day the administration announced that we would have a free day to wash our belongings and get prepared. We had never experienced such generosity before and surmised that such good treatment in the beginning promised only good for the future. We said good-bye to many prisoners. Three years of living together as we had makes people very close. I heard later that the administration of Userda deplored our transfer. Our proud camp commandant said that he would give a hundred other women for these eighteen political prisoners.

13

The Slow Road to Freedom

THE NEXT DAY we were put into open trucks
and taken to Irkutsk to the same transient prison I had
been in five years before. The political prisoners from
Userda were all Lithuanian and Ukrainian. We were put
into a cell so big we weren't crowded and were not expected
to work. This seemed to us like a vacation resort. The food
was not good but was sufficient since we were not working.
Every day new transports of prisoners, now only criminals,
arrived at the camp and soon our cell became crowded to
overflowing. Prisoners from other transient camps reported
that a big transportation of political prisoners was going on
all around. We expected something better to come from all
this upheaval.

After three weeks in transient prison, a convoy was called
consisting of our eighteen women and about forty hardened
criminals. Again we were all questioned—how long a sentence, what paragraph, how much time had been spent
already in prison.

We were amused at one Mongolian woman who was
supposed to be a political prisoner but when she was asked

why she was there she said for a cow. We all laughed. What did a cow have to do with politics? She said she had been a cow herder at the time the director of her collective farm stole a cow, sold it in the black market, and blamed her. When the controllers investigated her, she told the story as it really happened. Nothing was done to the director but in revenge he later made a political accusation against her, she was arrested and sentenced to ten years.

We were taken to a railroad station and put into cattle cars. This crowded journey resembled our tragic deportation but now there were only women, no sick or children, and a hole had been bored in the floor to serve us as toilet facilities. The car was so crowded that we couldn't sit or lie down. We had no blankets. We were ordered to put our luggage into a special compartment, which was a wise move, for otherwise the criminals would have stolen everything. An officer from Userda who accompanied us showed some concern for us and ordered the guards to build additional sleeping benches in the car so that we could all sit and sometimes lie down. We remained on the train for five days, again without any knowledge of where we were going. Food was brought to us twice a day but beyond that the guards didn't care what happened.

We had a lot of trouble with the criminals. At first they cursed and chased us. Since we were in the minority we stayed in one corner and kept as quiet as possible. We used our small handbags as pillows. One morning a few of us discovered that the handbags had been cut with a knife while we slept and everything had been stolen. We inquired about this very carefully but as a result even our drinking water was spoiled in revenge. The rest of the trip we never all slept at the same time but always had one awake to act as guard.

After five days we stopped at a small station. We were somewhere in the region of Taishet, still in Siberia. We saw big white houses nearby and knew that this was another camp. We were ordered to get out and stand in line with the criminal women. We got off but the prospect of living with such companions was so awful that we began to protest. We cried and told them to go ahead and shoot us but we wouldn't live with those women. The train was still standing there and the convoy leader said, "You can stay here, but you will lose all your belongings." I still had many good things in my luggage so I was the first to relent.

The camp commandant arrived and informed us that the camp was for invalid political prisoners, the criminals had been brought as domestic workers, and we would not be mixed with them.

The camp looked quite nice. It was quiet and decent and we were immediately conscious of a different atmosphere. Only the inmates made a bad impression. Most of them were very old, some were crippled, paralyzed or arthritic. Work in the prison camps had taken its toll.

We looked around trying to find some Lithuanians and we found two. One was still a young woman but very pale and bent. When I introduced myself she asked me if I was the Armonas from Rimgaudai, the name of our farm, neighbors of Krivickas. I nodded. She told me that she was Mrs. Krivickas, wife of the older son who was a leader in the freedom fighters. She had not been arrested until 1953 so she told me lots of things that had happened after I left.

In 1949 occurred an even larger deportation than in

1948. All farmers with large properties or leadership qualities disappeared. It was estimated that at least ten per cent of the total Lithuanian population went through the torture of deportation. She said that after that deportation, larger numbers of Soviet police and soldiers arrived and their stepped-up persecution completely eliminated the partisan resistance.

Her husband, she, and two young freedom fighters, seeing no sense in further resistance, went into hiding. In a Latvian forest about ten miles beyond the Lithuanian border they built a bunker big enough for them to be able to bake bread inside. They arranged with a Lithuanian farmer to bring them supplies a few times each year. In the winter they couldn't get out of the bunker while snow was on the ground for fear of leaving telltale footprints.

A brother of Krivickas was in hiding in a different place. He was secretly married to a Lithuanian girl named Zemelis who had a love affair with a Communist and betrayed her husband by telling his hiding place. He was found and killed. She knew the name of the farmer who was supplying food to the bunker and betrayed him too. When threatened by the secret police, the farmer led the police to the place in the forest and sounded the code. All four came out of the bunker to find themselves surrounded by police and soldiers. Mrs. Krivickas and another young fighter raised their hands when ordered to do so but her husband and the other young boy jumped back inside. They resisted until all their ammunition was gone and then blew themselves up rather than surrender. So died the last man of the tragic Krivickas family. Another son had been killed a few years earlier, Mr. Krivickas had died on the road, and Mrs. Krivickas had died shortly thereafter.

This girl was arrested, tortured, and beaten so badly by investigators who were trying to get from her information about other hiding places that she never recovered. After being sentenced to a twenty-five-year term she had been sent to this camp because her kidneys had been damaged.

The new camp was very different from the others. There were lectures and the prisoners were grouped according to their education, which seemed strange to us for no one had cared about such things anywhere else.

We did not have to work so I had lots of time to talk with other prisoners. I listened to stories about other camps and prisons and was thankful to have missed some of the really bad places.

Life in the "heavy regime" prisons and camps was many times worse than anything I had experienced. The prisoners wore numbers, they were never paid for their work, and after work they weren't free to go into the yards but were locked in their cells; even the food was worse. They were beaten and mistreated by sadistic guards. Much of the Russian and Siberian north was filled with such camps. The most famous ones were in the Kolima area. There are many songs in Russia about Kolima such as, "Be damned, Kolima, wonder place of this planet, if it happens to you to go there, there will never be a way back."

One Ukrainian girl who looked very young (she was then sixteen years old) told us a story from the Kolima area of a big uprising about ten months after the fall of Beria. She said that in the hard labor camp in which she was kept there were many prisoners who were important Russians such as officers or high officials. The plans to revolt were developed over many months and even weapons were smuggled into the camp. The revolting prisoners demanded more freedom, better food, and pay for the work as in the correction camps. The camp was surrounded by soldiers and the fighting went on for a long time. There were many casualties. When the camp surrendered and she was taken out with other women, they had to pass through a yard full of bodies. The leaders of the revolt were executed but later on conditions were much improved.

Some of the women, particularly those who had been in prison for more than ten years, told about the reign of terror of the criminals. It seemed that the idea of correction camps where prisoners are allowed freedom in the yards doesn't work with hard-core criminals. They not only ruled the prison on the inside and mistreated the political prisoners, but even managed to terrorize the entire camp administration. There were no open revolts but the criminals eliminated the officials they disliked; by rolling dice in secret sessions prisoners were selected to kill the chosen officer and thus to sacrifice themselves. Such criminal reigns had been famous about the time of my arrest. Afterwards, the more dangerous criminals were isolated in special camps and their influence was not so pronounced.

In a few days we were ordered to leave this camp although we all wanted to stay there. Julia, our tailor, was a smart and aggressive woman. She persuaded the administration to let her stay on as the camp tailor.

We were transported by train with only one guard, which made a favorable impression on us. We rode about sixty miles and stopped. We were told we were being sent to the political prison camp of Novociunka, which turned out to be not far from the railroad station. It looked gray and run down, everything was muddy, the camp area was dirty, and the houses and sleeping rooms were rough and poorly kept. Compared with the beauty of Userda we disliked this camp at first, but before long we became quite happy. This woman's camp had about five hundred inmates, among them at least 150 Lithuanians; the rest were Ukrainians and Germans. It was quiet and polite, no shouting, no cursing, no violence. Even the administration behaved differently. We began to feel almost like human beings again. The food was not bad. I liked the cabbage soup.

The camp had been established for the lumber industry but after the forest had been cleared, farming was started so Novociunka was now a small-scale Userda. Discipline was similar to Camp 104.

The day after our arrival we were set to scattering manure in the fields. After a few days we were given the harder jobs of spreading fertilizer. We had to walk only one mile to work, which was nothing to us, but the method of spreading fertilizer was enough to make up for that. There were no spreaders, so we were given straw bowls full of the fertilizer which were hung around our necks and were told to spread it with both hands. Each container weighed over forty pounds so it was not very long before we were miserable, especially the young girls and the weaker ones. The agricultural supervisor kept telling us it was a pity the work was so hard but he couldn't help it. The job must be done and he had no other way to do it.

There were constant rumors that screening boards were

working in various prisons and setting people free. A quarter mile away from Novociunka was a camp for men political prisoners. We were told that a screening team was working in that camp. We asked any official we found when the screening board would come to our camp. Our persistent questions became so annoying that anyone from the administration who was passing by started to shout, "I don't know when the board will be here," even before we could open our mouths.

Next we heard that the screening board had finished in the men's camp and was not coming to us but was moving to another camp a little farther away. We were afraid that if they did not come now, Russian laws, which changed so often, would be altered before we had any advantage from this wave of leniency. If another, severer set of laws was enacted, we might lose forever the chance of being released. In a strange way, all the women organized and decided not to work and to declare a strike because the screeners were not coming to our camp. In the old times such a strike would have been broken quickly but now the administration was uncertain and very lenient. They tried to persuade us to go back to work, but failed. Finally, the camp commandant promised that a representative from the screening committee would be there that evening and would hold a meeting with all the prisoners. After this promise we went to work. I was digging stumps out of the fields at the time.

That evening the meeting was held. The men from the board asked us the reason for our discontent. Each of us was afraid to be the first to talk. It was dangerous to show any quality of leadership no matter how small, so we all cried out together. Either we were all silent or we were all shouting and crying. We demanded to know why we were being put off. After a general discussion the men gave us their word of honor that the board would be back in one week. They kept their word.

A schoolhouse outside of our camp was prepared for the screenings. Our camp commandant called a meeting the day before the screenings were to start and advised us to admit our guilt if we were asked. He said that many of our prisoners would be released but that stubborn behavior could impair our chances.

In Novociunka there were about 140 women who were over seventy years old, mostly Lithuanians. They were the mothers of killed or captured freedom fighters and had been sentenced for their "children's sins." They were screened first and all were released.

Then each morning when we were in line to go to work, forty would be called out. After the process of investigation the decision was not announced on each case individually. At five P.M. all those who had been processed that day were called back and the formal decision concerning their release or detention was read. All the prisoners were in an indescribable state of mental anguish while waiting to hear their fate. Everyone hoped for the best but dared not feel too sure.

14

I Am Free

I WAS CALLED in the first group after the invalids because my name started with A. We were put, all forty of us, into a waiting room and one by one we were called to be screened. Two women among us were particularly nervous. One kept repeating under her breath that she would not be released. She had been caught while helping the Lithuanian partisans by carrying ammunition to them. The other woman, a Volga German, had worked in a German office in Russia as an interpreter. Once she helped a man get a job on the railroad, who was later arrested by the Germans, accused of being a Communist, and executed. She was then accused by the Russians of betraying the man, and she felt she had no chance at all.

I was one of the first to be called. Behind a long desk in the room sat twelve investigators. I was shaking all over. One of the men processing me asked the usual questions, what sentence, which paragraph, how many years already served. He didn't ask at all about my crimes, or demand any admission of guilt. He asked where my husband was, where my daughter was, did I know where my son was, and did I receive support from America. Finally he asked if

I still wanted to go to the United States. I said if I was released I would do everything in my power to reach my family. When I left the room I had a feeling that I would be released but until five that evening I lived in fearful suspense.

I asked the woman who had worked in the resistance movement how things had gone for her. She said that the investigator asked her if she supplied the partisans with ammunition and she said yes. Then he asked if she knew that human beings could be killed with that ammunition and she said yes again.

At five o'clock all forty of us stood silently and the chairman of the screening committee read the list.

"Barbara Armonas: Set free; constitutional rights restored."

On the way back to camp I didn't even feel the ground under my feet. All the way I repeated to myself, "I am free, I am free, I am free." I sat down to write a letter to John at once:

My dearests,

It has been a long time since I have been able to write to you. I was living under such conditions that I was unable to write, please forgive me. Today is one of the happiest days of my life. A few minutes ago a court order was read and it stated that I was being set *free*. For several moments I could not think straight, I cried and laughed with joy, but now at the same time my hands are shaking and I am almost unable to write.

There is so much I would like to write you. I want to express all the happiness a prisoner feels when he is given his freedom and also to tell you that freedom is worth more than anything else in the world. But then I know that you probably will not understand my greatest happiness since you have not been a prisoner, John.

Now that I am free, I do not have anywhere to go. I do not know whether I will be permitted to return to Lithuania since I have not received my written documents. Here in Siberia no one is waiting for me, nothing of mine is here. After such hard years I do not have a place to rest my tired head.

Nevertheless, I still am very lucky because I am going to visit Johnny and I will try to get permission to see him, and it will be the greatest happiness for him and me. It is very sad that you and Donna cannot share the happy hour with us. Tomorrow I will send a telegram to Johnny and inform him that I am free and then I will write to you, John, as soon as I am settled somewhere.

The next morning our camp cultural and propaganda leader tried to talk us into going to work as usual to show our gratitude to the Soviet Union which had treated us so generously. Some of the Ukrainian women went, but all of us from Lithuania refused. What could they do to us now?

I was declared free on June 13, 1956. The next day I put all my things in order, wrote letters to my son, and to my friends in Lithuania. I didn't know what to do, so decided to go to the Buriat Mongol area to Ulan-Ude and stay as close as possible to Johnny, perhaps try to get work at least until he finished his schooling. He had one more year in secondary school. I went with a group of others to the adjacent village where there was a post office. It was an unbelievable thrill to know that I was outside the camp and that no one was following me.

New transports of criminal prisoners and embezzlers were coming in. Anticipating that large numbers of prisoners would be released, the administration admitted more new prisoners than there were places available. They were crowded temporarily into the potato cellars and other similar places.

I do not believe the stories that prison camps have been completely eliminated in the Soviet Union. The number of political prisoners is smaller no doubt—in Novociunka no less than nine in ten were released—but what could they have done with the millions of embezzlers?

We waited a few days to be processed. Passports and tickets were issued to us. At first the screening board didn't orient themselves very well and were issuing tickets and permits to Lithuania. Perhaps I could have gotten such a ticket too if I had asked. Later the board found that release from prison didn't mean release from deportation and then wrote tickets only to the place at which the prisoner had been arrested.

I was given my new passport, a ticket to Mongolia, and fifty rubles' travel money. The issuing official told me, "I wish you luck," and that was the end of the state's concern with me.

The following day we were taken to a railroad station five miles from the camp. About two hundred people waited all night long for a train, not only from our camp but from others as well. In the Taishet area 350 miles east of Krasnoyarsk there were many prison camps.

I had trouble with my luggage. Nearly everyone had one

or two pieces but I had four. This station didn't handle baggage so I asked some girls from our group to help me. The train stopped only two minutes. There was a tremendous commotion as everyone tried to climb on at once. I noticed that one of my bags had been left. My friend, Mary, with whom I was traveling, jumped out to get the bag but the train started to move and she was left behind. Her belongings were all with me.

After a few hours of travel we arrived in Taishet. The station was so full of people that there was hardly a place to sit even on the floor. The next train wasn't expected from Novociunka for twenty-four hours but Mary managed to get on a freight and arrived earlier than I had expected. Since I was having such problems with my baggage, I decided to go home with her, which was on my way, and leave some things there for a while.

After waiting twelve hours longer, we got a train. As we were riding along the conductor told us that this train didn't stop in Mary's town. We passed her station and went on to the next one. We arrived early in the morning and the only man at the station told us that the highway was ten miles away. Since this was probably as close as we could expect to find transportation, we didn't know what to do.

The next village was two miles away so we picked up our six pieces of luggage and started walking. This soon became too much so we would put one piece down, carry the other two as far as we could while still keeping the first one in sight, then set those down and return for the first one. In this manner we leapfrogged into the village. After much searching we found a truck and a driver. We told him we were from prison, offered him good pay, and he agreed to take us to Mary's village. Admitting to having been in prison is no shame in Russia. Without exception the people are very helpful to former prisoners.

There was great joy in Mary's family because not only had she come home, but one of her brothers had arrived from prison the day before. The father and two other brothers worked in the coal mines. They had been well-to-do farmers in Lithuania, but now the whole family lived in one room in an old shack. I slept on the floor and the next day continued my journey to Ulan-Ude, taking only a few things with me.

I was fortunate in finding a truck that was going to Cheremkhovo, the place to which we had been deported. The station there was very crowded. I waited almost twenty-four hours to get a train to the border. It seemed that nothing had changed in the eight years since I had been there. The policeman went through the waiting rooms waking passengers and suggesting that they shouldn't sleep if they didn't want their things stolen.

I left Cheremkhovo in the early morning. We passed the mountainous and picturesque shore of the Lake Baikal and arrived at Ulan-Ude late in the afternoon, and fortunately for me, the train stopped directly at the entrance of the big military camp which was located in a sandy desert area.

15

Back to Lithuania with Johnny

I ASKED THE GUARD at the entrance to call Ivan Armonas. The guard couldn't find him so he allowed me to enter the camp and then I was told that Johnny was playing with the orchestra and wouldn't be home until two the next morning, but when I got to the building where he lived, the sergeant-at-arms told me he was there. I waited fifteen minutes before he came.

He looked much thinner and smaller than I had expected. He was sixteen. Our reunion was very touching. We started to talk and his officer, the orchestra leader, came into the room. He greeted me, extending his hand. This made quite an impression on me. In the eight years since being deported, no official had offered his hand to me. He asked if I had enough money to reach my destination and after exchanging a few more words he left the room.

Now I asked Johnny what I should do. Once before we had made a fatal error in not fleeing to Germany when the Russian armies approached. Again I faced a hard decision. I had intended to stay here in Mongolia near Johnny for a year until he finished his schooling. I had made a firm decision to get a good education for him somehow. After secondary school we would see what could be done about the future.

Johnny told me, "Mama, you must go back to Lithuania where you have all your friends and relatives. Life here is very hard. There are sand storms and it is terribly hot in summer. Except for the glass factories there is hardly any work available and I hear that working conditions in those factories are very hard."

The next morning we went to Ulan-Ude to buy materials to pack all my things in the way required by the baggage rules in Russia. We took a taxi from the base to the city and had lunch in a restaurant. I hadn't been in a taxi since 1944.

I knew I was running a big risk by going back to Lithuania when my release papers were made for Mongolia. Johnny talked to his supervisors who were very considerate and gave him the maximum possible military leave, forty-five days. When they issued his free round-trip ticket there was a notation on it that his mother was accompanying him.

The next day we started our trip. The notation on his ticket permitted us to buy my ticket at the soldiers' window. The lines for private tickets were a hundred yards long and otherwise we would have spent at least a half day waiting there.

We rode to Cheremkhovo and from there to the village where Mary lived. We got to Mary's at night, knocked on the door, and Mary gave us beds on the floor. After spending a half day with this friendly family we resumed our journey. There was a group of Lithuanian deportees on our train who had obtained permits to return. It seemed that not only political prisoners were being released but some deportees were also able to get permits to return home.

After five days of travel in the overcrowded train we reached Moscow. The small discomforts we encountered meant nothing to me now. I had been well trained in hardship. We changed stations in Moscow and had a little time to look around. At last I saw a really luxurious subway station. It made me see clearly the difference of the standard of living between the capital of Soviet Russia and the poor collective farms and the various kinds of labor camps.

The journey from Moscow to the Lithuanian capital of Vilnius was quick. We almost overslept. We and our traveling companions stopped in Vilnius to visit the historic churches (many of which had been turned into museums and storehouses). One very religious woman came back after finding one still open for worship and told me, "Do you know, for ten years I haven't been to a religious service."

We decided to go first to the farm on which I was born, where relatives were living. I had written them that I was coming so after a few hours more travel, and three times longer waiting in stations for transfers, we came to the town of Pasvalys.

I was surprised. Pasvalys didn't seem in bad condition and lots of new buildings were going up. But our small village made quite a different impression. All the big shade trees were gone, there were no fences around our property or around the neighbors' property. Everything was terribly run down. It looked as if a big tornado had hit there within the past six months. The houses were standing but the stables and barns were half torn down.

My great desire had been to show my birthplace to my son. He didn't remember anything about Lithuania. I had talked about the many flowers which surrounded every Lithuanian farmhouse, but now even flowers were scarce, and somehow the sight of the house didn't elate me as I had expected it to. It all looked strange and foreign. So many things had happened to me that I felt remote from everything.

I saw a relative of mine working in a garden near our home. She was surprised to see me so soon and our unexpected homecoming was very warm. We stayed there for two days, exchanging all the news of things that had happened during the eight years I had been gone.

First I was told the tragic story of my younger brother. They hadn't written me about it while I was in prison because they didn't want to cause me any additional grief. In 1944 my brother was taken into the Russian Army and later arrested for some unknown reason and sentenced to ten years in prison without the privilege even of writing letters. It was possible that he had tried to desert. The supply situation was so bad that there was often only a choice of staying and starving or deserting and, possibly, surviving. Perhaps he had said something against Communism—who knows?

In 1949 a truckload of prisoners had passed through Pasvalys. It stopped for a short time and one of the prisoners shouted to a passer-by, "This is Pasvalys, do you know Jonas Balciunas? Tell his friends and relatives that a few months ago he died of malnutrition in Riga prison."

Despite my experiences, I hadn't lost my fighting spirit. The tragedy of my brother upset me very much. What kind of government wouldn't even bother to advise relatives of their victims' death? We still don't know for sure what had happened to him. Perhaps the prisoner was not telling the truth or perhaps the message was distorted.

I was surprised at the apathy of the relatives and friends with whom I talked. They spoke about the victims of shootings, deportations, or prisons with the same resignation as of friends who had died from cancer or heart attacks.

I noticed, too, that our people, like the people in Russia, had stopped talking about politics. I tried many times to ask about the resistance against Communism, but even my close friends always changed the subject to simple everyday problems.

Despite the cordial reception I received, I felt that my relatives were worried about what I would do. They couldn't afford an extra burden and I had no money, no job, and my health was poor.

From Pasvalys we went to see our farm. It was terribly run down. Our modern flax barn was completely wrecked. Broken parts of the machines were still lying around the yard. The shingled roofs of our barns had rotted; the holes had been patched with handfuls of straw to prevent leaking. There were no fences standing. We had planted a young orchard with sixty apple and pear trees. Only five trees remained. Our main house had been completely neglected.

I was warmly greeted by the family now living in the house. There was nothing left of our old furniture. The people asked me to stay with them and kept repeating, "Just tell us when you want to move in to your own property, we will let you in."

In talking with friends and relatives in my native village and around our farm, I learned that big changes had taken place. Everything was now under collective farming. After the big deportations of 1948 and 1949 and the complete collapse of the partisans' resistance, a drive was started in the autumn of 1949 to have everyone join the collective farms. This was supposed to be voluntary but really all the farmers were forced to hand over everything they had; farm equipment; all animals except one cow, one pig, and a certain amount of poultry; all resources in seed, animal foods, and the like. No one was paid. Next, all the farmers were put to work in collective work gangs where everyone supposedly had equal rights. Each gang was under a supervisor called a brigadier who kept a record of their performance. The chairman of the collective and other officials were supposed to be elected by the farmers, but in reality they were appointed by the local chairman of the Communist Party.

The idea of belonging to the collectives was very unpopular. Everyone tried to hide as much of his goods as he could. Pigs and cattle were slaughtered, harnesses and tools were hidden by burying them or dropping them into ponds and even now, after seven years, the collective organization sometimes found hidden horse carriages or similar items and confiscated them.

The farmers resisted collectivization by all possible means but to no avail. I heard the story of one of my neighbors named Mazeika. He and his wife, who had no children, lived on their ten-acre farm. They were industrious and managed to live well. They opposed the collective farming and since they had never had any hired workers, they didn't belong to the class called "kulakh" which is a general term for rich farmers who not only worked themselves but had hired farm hands. Mazeika didn't belong to any political organizations so there was no official reason for persecution. The land all around them was already collective but still the family refused to join. They were forced to pay heavy taxes which they somehow managed to meet. The next year the same heavy taxes were levied and again they paid. Finally, the collective administration ordered the tractor operators to plow across their lands; such a good example of successful resistance could not be allowed. When the tractor started across the land, Mrs. Mazeika ran to the field and threw herself in its path. The driver didn't know what to do, and retired. The next day both Mr. and Mrs. Mazeika were taken to secret police headquarters for questioning. What happened there was never found out, but they gave up their resistance and joined.

Officially all farmers are members of the collective farms as co-owners but in reality they work as the administration orders. The farmers are paid for their work only after the crops are in and after the government has received its quota. The price the government paid then was low. For a hundred pounds of grain the farmers received four rubles, although the same amount in the free market brought 180 rubles. After the government took its quota at the official price, and all collective executives had received their salaries, what remained was divided between the workers according to the number of days they had spent in the fields. In general, this amounted to one or two rubles per working day, plus about two pounds of grain. In American money this amount of cash and goods would equal approximately twenty-five cents per day. The farmers survive and feed their families from their private gardens, which average an acre and a half, and from the privilege of keeping a cow, a pig, and some poultry. Even from their gardens they must turn in a quota of grain and meat and deliver about half of the milk from their cows. The farmer is forced to work six days a week in the fields of the collective and can work in his own garden only on Sunday or at night. It is difficult to get a horse to plow his garden. He must pay for this or often even bribe the supervisors. Without a horse he finds it almost impossible to go to market or to church.

There has been a new law issued by the Khrushchev government stating that if a collective farmer and his wife do not work a certain minimum number of days in the fields, his garden will be confiscated. This law says that only two tenths of an acre of land cannot be taken from him. This threat works better than the methods used during Stalin's time when a non-worker was declared a saboteur and imprisoned.

The farmers would like to escape from such working conditions but they are not permitted to leave the farm without an official release which is given only if a man is sent to prison, enters the army, or goes away to study. It seems to me that the whole idea is for the government to get as much as possible in farm production without paying for it.

One friend told me that Soviet Russia has invented nothing new. In Czarist times the Russian aristocracy played a big part in the world while the farmers lived on next to nothing. Now the new Russia impresses the world with missiles, military strength, and luxurious buildings in certain selected cities. The seventy million poor farmers pay for all this, but who cares about them? All they need is enough strength to plow the land and milk the cows. If the farm areas are sealed off from foreign newspapermen, everything looks rosy and progressive. No one from abroad is allowed to travel in Lithuania, except in the capital city.

All my old friends who trusted me complained with tears in their eyes. They felt that their grandparents as serfs a hundred years ago had better living standards than they. At least then everyone had a horse and worked only a hundred days a year for the landlord. Now they were being fed a constant stream of propaganda about happy living on the collective farms and their freedom from capitalistic exploitation.

It was a shame to see such exploitation of the farmers because, since Lithuania is primarily a farming country, this means exploitation of nearly the entire population. Despite strict controls and forced organization, the collective farms were not successful. In the neighborhood of our farm there had been many prosperous and rich farmers, yet now everyone was poor. Somehow, these collective farms reminded me of Userda Camp.

A few large families with sons who have better-paying jobs, such as tractor drivers, have a decent life. Surprisingly, even the poorer families still have parties and try to dress as well as they can. There is no incentive to save because savings that can't be used to improve one's living standard are useless; therefore everything is consumed at once for immediate pleasure.

All of the houses are run down because the people have no time or means with which to fix them. The administration is concerned only with fulfilling the government requirements and distinguishing themselves as good productive leaders. The government strongly encourages people to leave their homes and go to live in community colonies. Though the farmers are offered loans and support, nearly everyone hopes that a change will come and that they may regain their property if they stay on it, so they are unwilling to change.

I spent a few days on our farm and the more I heard about the collectives the worse that life looked to me. When they couldn't talk about the situation the farmers expressed their feelings in many folk songs ridiculing the system and describing their hardships.

The chairmen of the collectives live well. They even have private cars and represent themselves as being very important persons. I didn't see the chairman of the collective that our farm now belonged with, but the woman living in our house said that she had told him I was back and would like to have my house. He answered her, "Oh, she is not such an important person. If she wants to work she is welcome, but we will find another shack for her."

While I was there, I inquired from the officials of our county about the possibility of regaining my farmhouse. The head official, who had a luxurious office, suggested that I write a petition. I visited an attorney to ask his advice and after I told him my story he said there was no hope at all. A few deportees had come back before me and made petitions, but no one had been successful. I was not only a deportee but had also been a political prisoner so he advised me not to waste the effort.

However, I had already almost made up my mind. I knew the only way to get my house back was to become a worker in the collective and I knew I didn't have the strength to work a garden and spend over 250 days on the farm just to survive.

When I got home I had had a letter from my husband. He wanted me to do everything possible to get a permit to go to America and even asked me, "Do you have a desire to come or not? Why do you do nothing?" I knew there was no way to explain the conditions to him, he couldn't possibly understand. I had just returned from prison. I was not registered and really had no right even to be in Lithuania, so how could I dare to risk my freedom by starting to make such improper demands?

There was still over a week of Johnny's leave left, so we spent the time traveling through Lithuania and visiting our friends and relatives. I must admit that considerable progress was being made in public transportation. We could travel anywhere in comfortable buses at very reasonable fares. We found that people who worked in the cities but lived in the suburbs and had their own gardens and cows, did not do badly. But one relative of mine who had been an official in Pasvalys and now lived in western Lithuania on a collective farm had nothing at all. He couldn't even offer us a decent meal. He had been approached by the secret police in Pasvalys and asked to be an informer. They thought he would be useful to them because he sang in the church choir. He refused, lost his job, and was even forced to find another place to live.

Finally the day for Johnny's departure came. I went to Vilnius with him. His train left at midnight and since I had no friends in the city and had no registration or travel permit and so couldn't register at a hotel, I spent the night in the railroad waiting room. The next morning I wandered around the city. It was as beautiful as ever. The damages of war had been repaired, there were many new houses, and I noticed that almost half of the people on the street now spoke the Russian language. In 1946 it was seldom indeed that you met a person who spoke Russian.

A friend in Pasvalys had told me about a Mrs. Miklase-vicius in Vilnius who was also trying to get a permit to join her husband and son in the United States, and had given me her address. When she opened the door and I spoke to her, telling her why I had come, she believed me and was friendly. It is seldom nowadays that anyone will trust you without a long acquaintance but I must have been convincing. She advised me to go to an office of the Internal Ministry.

An official there looked at my pass and immediately asked why I was not registered. I could have been arrested but I explained that I had just arrived from Russia, so he gave me a stern warning and then advised me to write to John for affidavits and then make my application. After that I returned to Pasvalys and decided to settle there for the time being, at least.

16

I Settle Down

In order to register you must first have a job. I tried in the factories and hospitals but couldn't get anything. Then I tried to find a room. Though it was possible to get a private room the price was high, over eighty rubles a month, twice as much as an apartment in a state-owned house. Finally, I did find a tiny room hardly large enough to hold a bed, for only twenty rubles. But I couldn't take it until I had a permit to settle.

I went to the city office and saw the director, a woman Communist named Liaugaudas. She was extremely unpleasant and almost threw me out, saying they didn't need any more of my kind, just go on back to Siberia. Outside, however, a clerk approached me to ask how much I would pay for the permit to settle. I agreed to give him five hundred rubles, one old dress, and one American Parker pen. With the new official permit and the registration book of the house where I had my room, I went to the police to be registered. They stamped my pass and I was safe again. I was terrified that they might ask for my other papers, for if I had been forced to show my release from prison they would have found my destination marked Mongolia, and would have refused to register me. But now I was a legal citizen. The pass with the registration stamp on it is a very important document to any Soviet citizen. Without it you can be arrested immediately, so I guarded it with my life.

I couldn't get into my room immediately because it wasn't ready, so I went visiting my friends and relatives again. I bought a summer overcoat for 160 rubles, silently thanking John for supporting me so generously. His wonderful parcels allowed me to exist without hard work and, in fact, without them I could never have paid the five-hundred-ruble train fare from Ulan-Ude. I was indeed a fortunate woman.

I attended some gay parties such as baptisms and engagement announcements. At one party I was among the first to arrive and was asked about my experiences so I started talking about Novostroika and prison. Everyone became very depressed until the host complained that he had invited people to be gay and not sad.

When I returned to Pasvalys I found three letters from John. He wrote that he would support me as well as he could and asked me not to take a job but to rest and recover. I moved into my small room and started again to acquire dishes and other necessities. I remembered that I had twice lost everything, once by deportation and again by arrest, and wondered how successful I would be this time. I had very little hope that I would be released to go to America. I planned to build my life about my son. I lived as quietly as possible. I went to my relatives in my old home occasionally to help them with their gardens, I wrote letters to my numerous friends from prison, but spent most of the time at my hobby of needlework. In October I received the necessary affidavits from America and went again to Vilnius. It was hard to find an attorney who would help me with all the necessary papers. They were all afraid to support anyone trying to leave the Soviet Union to go to a capitalist country. I finally found one who would handle the many papers required. I was required to describe my life, in detail, and that of all my relatives for the last twenty years. My attorney, to whom I paid five hundred rubles, worked with me nearly four days.

During this time something very important happened. While I was in Vilnius there was open revolt in Hungary. Everyone was extremely excited and thought surely there would be a general war but no one was afraid, even of the possibility of atomic assault. Secretly we all listened to the Voice of America and other translated broadcasts. You could feel the excitement as you walked along the streets. In Kaunas the students organized a demonstration in the cemetery where Lithuanian soldiers were buried. They started making speeches but this was broken up, over a hundred of the demonstrators were arrested, and many of them were sentenced to ten years in prison. Despite fifteen years of Communist education and careful screening, the spirit of freedom is still alive in Lithuanian students.

The tragic outcome of the Hungarian revolution was a terrible disappointment to everyone. Now we felt there was no shred of hope that the West would help us to rid our countries of the hated occupation.

I went home and spent a quiet winter. At Christmas time I fell sick and tried to get medical care which was now free to everyone. During independent times we had had three doctors in Vabalnikas; now there were more than ten.

There were three hospitals and ambulances for both the city and farming area, yet when I went to see a doctor I found long lines waiting to get in. I thought I would return the next day earlier in the morning but even then the long lines were patiently waiting. A nurse came out, chose a few people and declared that that was all for the day. The same thing happened on the third day. Someone told me that in Panevezys there were a few doctors who had the right to charge a fee so I went there and got a doctor without difficulty.

Because medicine is free and everyone who goes to a doctor is released from work, many more wait in line than there are really sick people. It is especially hard to reach a doctor who has a high reputation or is a famous specialist. Everyone knows that the only way to secure service is to make a gift in advance to the doctor or his receptionist. The advantages of such a system are only for the important people, who get the best specialists free and without waiting.

Johnny came home in the spring. He had finished secondary school and since he wanted to be released from the orchestra he was permitted to come to Pasvalys permanently. He had papers from the camp listing his destination as Pasvalys so he had no difficulty in registering. He was asked only what his mother was doing and he told them, working as domestic help.

Meanwhile the answer had come from the Minister of the Department of the Interior; my application for an exit visa had been rejected.

I had decided to send my son through college if it could be arranged so I now inquired about the possibility of his

studying in Lithuania. He needed a letter of recommen-
dation from the local youth party organization, one from the
local party organization, and one from the director of his
school. It was very difficult to get a study permit unless you
were a Communist and completely impossible if the parents
were political prisoners or kulakhs.

Therefore, since there was no possibility for Johnny to
get further education in Lithuania, he decided to go to
Leningrad to study engineering. In the college where he
applied, there were over eight hundred applicants and only
two hundred openings. He spent two months there, passed
the examinations but was not accepted because there were
two hundred applicants with higher grades. He came back
to Pasvalys and we spent the winter together, while he
studied mathematics and physics and took lessons in the
Lithuanian language with one of the local teachers. There
was no place for him in my room so he got a permit to
sleep in the room of the house owner and spend the days
with me. I told him to be as quiet as possible, not to attend public meetings, and not to get involved in anything.

John wrote to me again and sent another set of affidavits.
He wanted me to make a new application for an exit visa.
When I went back to the Pasvalys police to start the new
procedure, they looked at my papers and said that the
application had just been refused; why did I want to start
again? I told them there was no harm in trying.

I went to Vilnius, found another attorney, and again
went through the routine of filling out all the papers. The
rules had been changed and the papers when completed
were to be submitted through the Pasvalys police. They
checked my political reliability on the local level, which

took them three months, before sending the papers on for further processing.

Every day it became harder to get Johnny the much-desired study permit. The only way to make a better life in the Soviet Union was through education, so the competition was keen for every available opening. We decided that he should try to study forestry. It looked promising because a forester could have his own garden and keep a cow.

The nearest Russian institute of forestry was in the city of Briansk between Smolensk and Moscow. Johnny went there and again competition was keen. For seventy-five openings there were over nine hundred applicants. On his political questionnaire Johnny said his father was unknown and his mother had been in prison as an embezzler. It was impossible for him to deny that his mother had been in prison because the fact was in his records from Ulan-Ude. We thought it was safer to admit his mother's imprisonment as an embezzler than as a political person. He was registered directly from Buriat Mongolia.

In August of 1958 he received a letter from the school saying that he had passed the examination and would be admitted. This gave us much joy because Johnny was already of military age and was being processed for induction into the army. On presenting proof of his admission, his induction was suspended until he finished school.

The political climate was now a little easier. People were no longer afraid to write letters to America, even to relatives who had gone there as refugees, though this may not have been true for people who had kept important positions. Parcels could be received from America without fear. There were no more big secret deportations and mass disappearances in the night. Apparently the Russians found that they could keep the population in line without harsh reprisals. People were still afraid to citicize Communism but an ordinary citizen caught at this for the first time would not be arrested. He could, however, lose his job, and have difficulty getting a new one. Influential people who were caught as anti-Communists still were treated with old-time Stalinist ruthlessness.

Some deportees were permitted to return to Lithuania from Siberia but their situation was not enviable. They had overwhelming difficulties in getting permits to settle and register. I heard that in the big cities it took a bribe of thousands of rubles to be registered and where could these poor people get that kind of money? It was also hard for them to get jobs, especially for the elderly. A few got their houses back but only if special boards decided that they had been illegally deported, and those few had friends or relatives with good positions in the Lithuanian Communist government. Other Lithuanians hesitated to show sympathy to returned deportees for fear they would be accused of sympathizing with kulakhs. In any case, no one was much concerned about these poor, weak, run-down, and now unimportant people.

Still people tried if possible to stay in Lithuania because life was better than in Russia, not so drab, and the food supply was better. But in many cases they were unable to settle and get jobs and were forced to return to Siberia.

The Communists now blamed Stalin for unnecessary cruelties. Thousands of victims were indeed being released from prisons but no one attempted to do anything to help them or to make up in any fashion for the suffering they had gone through; their persecution goes on even yet. Their children cannot study in the universities, and they are not eligible for the pension plan for the old.

My husband wrote me optimistic letters about the prospects for my release. He said that many important Americans were kindhearted and gave their support to our case but I didn't believe him and told my friends that I hoped those people would continue to try to help until I died.

At the end of August my son went to Briansk to enter school. After a few weeks a letter from him reported that all students had to spend one month getting agricultural experience and that he was working on a collective farm near Briansk. He was surprised at the poor organization of work on the farm. For instance, more than half the potato crop was left in the ground because the work norms were based on the number of furrows gone over rather than the total amount of potatoes harvested. He also said that the discipline was much less strict than anything he had seen in Lithuania. The workers didn't appear before noon and the buildings were even more run down and shabby than on Lithuanian farms. There were no toilet facilities, inside or out.

He sent me a questionnaire which I was to fill out; where his parents worked, did they own property, and so on. This questionnaire had to be confirmed by the local government. I dressed as poorly as possible and went to the chief of the government of Pasvalys asking him to confirm what I had written. He started then to question me. Where did I work? Where did I live? When I told him that I was a casual worker he reprimanded me and asked why I didn't go to a collective farm or into the building industry. I said it was hard to get a job and he told me that in the Soviet Union there were no unemployed people. After some wrangling I got him to sign the papers but with a warning to get my employment situation in order.

For fear that my record of unemployment might harm Johnny, I decided to look for a steady job. I found work as a domestic housemaid, cooking and caring for the small baby of a young couple who both worked in the local state bank. They earned about eight hundred rubles a month and paid me one hundred rubles plus my meals. I didn't need the money for I could make enough by selling the goods from the parcels which John sent me. For a woman's scarf which sells in the United States for fifty or sixty cents, I could get sixty to eighty rubles, almost my entire month's wages.

The job gave me comparative freedom, however, which meant a lot to me, and the work was not physically difficult. Most important for me was the record of my membership in the labor union which testified that I was working steadily.

Johnny received a scholarship amounting to 290 rubles a month. He couldn't live on this amount but I helped by sending him about 150 rubles a month and food parcels, and he made a little more by playing in a dance band in the evenings.

I was called to the local police office and questioned again. They asked me why I wanted to leave the Soviet Union, asked about my prison term, what paragraph I was sentenced under, how I lived now, if I had an apartment. For a few days after this I tried to guess what this questioning meant for my future. Perhaps it was in connection with my new application for a visa.

My excitement had not yet quieted down when a strange man came to me one day and asked me to sell him American money. He said an acquaintance of mine had told him that I got lots of parcels and goods from America and perhaps my husband was sending me money secretly as well. He offered me twenty-five rubles for a one-dollar bill, thirty-five rubles per dollar for a five, and forty rubles per dollar for larger denominations. I was surprised that he would offer such rates, considering the tourist exchange was ten rubles and the official exchange four rubles on the dollar. I was impressed too by his boldness in coming and asking openly. At first I thought he must be an informer but later I was convinced that he was nothing more than a black market businessman.

The black market is a very important part of everyday life in the Soviet Union. The Communist government was able to eliminate all political opposition, they even succeeded in suppressing and nearly eliminating the religious influence among the masses, but despite intense efforts from the beginning to abolish the black market, they have not been successful. The most active part of economic life goes on outside the legal market. Desirable goods disappear promptly from the government stores and reappear at much higher prices in the black market. Structural materials are stolen from big government construction sites and later sold in the black market so that small private houses spring up like mushrooms. All government workers dealing in goods, permits, and licenses, try to exploit this situation and make extra money. All who work in production, storerooms, or sales organizations, live conspicuously better than those who have no contact with the flow of goods or money.

I spent a quiet winter, my husband and son wrote often but there was no evidence that we would one day be together. I received word from the police that my application for an exit visa had again been rejected.

In the early spring we had some excitement. It was announced that a Communist delegation from Canada would visit Pasvalys. The collective farm to which my birthplace belonged, now called "Atzalynas," was selected as a showplace for the visitors. A few weeks before the delegation was to arrive, the beautification and cleaning of the farm commenced. Windows were replaced, painting done, fences mended. A special board selected the best cattle from the neighborhood and the day before the visit the cattle were put into the collective stables. The people didn't have much opportunity to talk with the visitors but nevertheless enjoyed themselves because during that day all dining places and cafeterias in Pasvalys lowered their prices way down to the official rates though usually they charged black market prices.

My son came home on vacation in the summer. I left my job for a few weeks and we spent the summer traveling in Lithuania and visiting friends and relatives.

On September 12, when Johnny had left for school, a Russian clerk came to tell me that I must go immediately to the secret police. I was terrified. I quickly burned all the letters from my husband. I had a few dollars and I hid them in the attic. I thought I would be searched and maybe arrested again. I was questioned about my life during deportation and in prison. They asked me how many

relatives had obtained and remailed letters to me from
America. I told them that everything had been legal, that
the camp censor controlled my letters. They said this was
not true, that no one controls letters in the Soviet Union,
that this was a fundamental freedom.

They asked me about Johnny and I told them that he
was studying in Briansk. This excited them. They didn't
understand how he had the right to study; after all, his
father was in America and we had been rich farmers. Then
they decided that perhaps it was because he had been in
a children's detention home and had no connection with
me. That would change things. I lost my patience at this
and asked my interrogator to explain to me why we were
being persecuted and why my son had no right to study.
When we had been farmers and had employed people to
help on our farm we had worked alongside them, and paid
and treated them well. Now I was a domestic worker who
was not well paid, working for a family of clerks for the
Soviet Union—why were they not persecuted for employing
people, as we were being persecuted for having had employees? My investigator was embarrassed and couldn't find
a ready explanation. He finally told me that my employers
worked for the government building Communism while
we had been working for our own personal gain.

I immediately wrote to Johnny urging him not to admit
to anyone that he knew anything about his father and to
be very careful. My greatest hope was that he could finish
his schooling.

On September 14 Khrushchev went to America. This
was much talked about. Some people argued, carefully and
secretly, that it was shameful for the leader of a cruel

dictatorship and the oppressor of small nations to be accorded red-carpet treatment in the stronghold of democracy. Others thought that it might have good results, that perhaps the Soviet Union would be encouraged in their program towards greater freedom for the people after Khrushchev had improved relations with the United States. We all began listening to the Voice of America which was no longer being jammed, at least temporarily. The jamming had been so successful that almost everyone had given up trying to get news from abroad.

On September 22 while listening to the Lithuanian Hour on the Voice of America, I became very much excited when I heard that in Iowa Mr. Khrushchev had promised to release the children of Mr. Leonas.

17

The Khrushchev Promise

THE NEXT EVENING my landlord came to see me excitedly and said, "Your name was mentioned. Your daughter talked to Mr. Khrushchev in Pittsburgh about you and your son." He and a close neighbor congratulated me but I had had too many disappointments. Until I heard it myself I brushed it off as impossible.

The next day I did hear it on a re-broadcast in the Lithuanian language. A few days later I received a telegram from John and a week after this a big letter came filled with clippings from the Cleveland *Press* and other newspapers describing my fate and telling of my daughter's talk with Mr. Khrushchev.

Mr. Khrushchev had told her, "Don't cry, little girl, your mother will join you."

Now I couldn't keep my door closed, hundreds of my acquaintances visited me. Letters came from all over the country, many from my circle of special friends. I was very proud of Donna. I didn't pay much attention to the story that my daughter had kissed Mr. Khrushchev's hand. When one of my friends mentioned it to me, another answered,

"So what? I would kiss K in any place if he would allow me to leave."

I went to visit some friends in Birzai to discuss the situation. We decided that I must go to Vilnius and Moscow and try to get all my papers, basing my efforts on Mr. Khrushchev's promise. I quit my job. The young couple were very unhappy because they couldn't get other help to run their house for the money they were paying me.

First I went to the Internal Ministry at Vilnius to inquire again at the Application Office. A Lithuanian clerk started to yell at me. When I showed him the clippings from the American newspapers he looked very serious and took the clippings to his superior, a Russian. This man told me, "If Nikita Sergejevich promised, he will do it. I wish you good luck in Moscow."

I reached Moscow by train without difficulty but as I had no travel papers, it was a problem to find a place to stay. After a lot of running around, I got into a hotel in the suburbs, sharing a room with four strangers. I went to the office set up to help Lithuanians in Moscow and it was the same story: at first they were cool but after seeing the clippings, particularly from the Cleveland *Press*, they showed an interest and I was interviewed by the head of the office. He said anything was possible, perhaps I would get a permit to leave.

I said I wanted an audience with Mr. Khrushchev. He thought this would be impossible but advised me to go to a special office in the Kremlin where petitions of citizens were accepted. I went there and put in my application. They told me that the answer would come by letter and advised me to go home and wait. I went to the Internal Ministry in Moscow and made application to Mr. Khrushchev and to the Minister of the Exterior, Mr. Gromyko.

Since I still had a little time to spend in Moscow, I decided to go to the Stalin and Lenin Mausoleum. I had an intense desire to see the body of the man who was personally responsible for so much suffering. I passed his casket in a long line of visitors, thinking that he could have been drowned by my own tears which had been shed over the years.

From Moscow I went to Briansk to see Johnny and tell him the good news. We talked together in the dormitory where he slept with twelve other students and decided that he should leave school immediately if an encouraging report came from Moscow. I asked him not to tell anyone of the Khrushchev incident. Only the Lithuanian people who listened to the Voice of America knew about the meeting. The Russian papers and radio hadn't mentioned it so no one in Briansk had heard the story.

I went back to Pasvalys and waited impatiently. Weeks passed and no word came from Moscow. On November 10 I was again called by the police. I was asked where I was born, where my son was, and all the rest of the old personal data. I asked if this questioning was in connection with my petition. They said they didn't know but repeated, "If Khrushchev promised, he will do it."

My husband wrote impatient letters urging me to fight as hard as I could but I didn't know what more to do. The Voice of America reported that the Leonas children were leaving for America. My husband sent their address in Vilnius which their parents in Chicago had given him. I went to Vilnius to find out what channels they had followed; perhaps I had slipped somewhere.

The Leonas daughter was afraid to talk with me. I waited a whole day but she was not at home. The next day I decided to wait in the hall as long as necessary. Finally she came, and when I told her my story she trusted me. I found that she had done nothing more than I, so I went home again to wait.

At this time all the movie houses were showing films of Khrushchev's travels through the United States. These played to overflowing crowds, everyone went more than once and I went three times. The people were not going to see Mr. Khrushchev, however, but to see the background and try to judge from what they could see just how things really were in America.

At Christmas time I went to visit my relatives and asked my landlord to send me a telegram if anything happened. The second day after Christmas a telegram came. I was to go to the police and fill out an application for a visa. The head of the police was now very kind to me. The pictures of my son were not of the proper size and were rejected, but the chief helped by accepting an enlargement of a picture taken from a group photograph.

Now I waited for news from the American Embassy in Moscow. Time dragged. My one desire was to get everything settled as fast as possible and get out. I was afraid that at any moment something would change and the opportunity would be lost.

Finally, on February 16, I received a telegram from the Embassy saying that a letter with a questionnaire and instructions had been mailed to me. Now everyone around was sure that I would soon be leaving.

My friends gave a farewell party for me. About thirty people came and because the group was large, the guests were afraid to talk. They all made farewell speeches wishing me good luck and expressing their joy that I was to join my family at last. No one mentioned that I was going to a land of democracy and freedom or that I would live in better conditions in the future. This was too dangerous. Only one remarked that if I should find myself with nothing to eat I must write them and they would send a few pounds of bacon. This ironical comment caused long and loud laughter.

My son now left his school and came home. Finally I received the letter from the Embassy. The instructions said that we must have X-ray pictures, blood tests, smallpox vaccinations, and several lesser items. We got the X-rays quickly but the blood tests were harder. The Pasvalys administration sent blood samples to the regional center of Panevezys for testing, but only every two weeks. We couldn't wait that long and went directly to Panevezys. The laboratory there would not accept us because we were from Pasvalys. It took a long time and much running around getting friends to help us before we overcame this obstacle.

Unfortunately the weather was bad, with big snowstorms which stopped all public transportation. We had only one thing in mind—faster, faster, as soon as possible; therefore, we hired a car to take us the eighty miles back to Vilnius. This cost five hundred rubles. We arrived in Vilnius on February 26, Friday. Again we ran into difficulties, this time in getting smallpox vaccinations, but with the help of friends we managed this too.

I was met with unusual interest in Vilnius, not only by friends and relatives; even unknown people came to see me, wishing me good luck and asking me to greet their relatives living in the United States.

I will never forget the visit of one old-time Lithuanian Communist, an old acquaintance of mine. At first I was afraid even to listen to what he was saying, thinking that this might be a trick to keep us from leaving. I still couldn't believe that I actually would be released and was suspicious of everything that happened, making mountains out of molehills in my efforts to do nothing that could give the government an opportunity to detain me. I didn't believe they would release me for I had seen so much and could tell so much from first-hand experience that would contradict their propaganda. I kept thinking that in some manner they would try to silence me.

However, this man seemed to be so sincere that I listened to him. He told me to tell the Americans that if things continued in the same way, soon only a few Lithuanians would remain, some in folk dance groups and some in the Lithuanian-language opera to show the world what a happy country this was, and a few shabby collective farmers. Even the official statistics show that there are now eight hundred thousand fewer Lithuanians than if the average national growth of independent times had continued. That means a lot for a nation of under three million people.

I asked him why he was telling me all this; I said he should choose someone better educated and more important. He felt that no important Lithuanian would ever be released from the Soviet Union. I then asked why he didn't send this message to Lithuanian refugees living abroad, but he said that these people already had lived there so long that no one paid much attention to them any more.

He went on to say that thirty years ago when he joined the Communist Party he never dreamed that it was a diabolically clever scheme to spread Russian international imperialism. Always before, politicians who worked hand in hand with the occupation authorities of a foreign power were called simple traitors, now they were called members of the Communist Party. This not only saves the faces of those who betray their country for their own personal gain, but helps to cheat the whole free world.

What would Americans call those citizens who, in case of American occupation by a foreign power, helped to eliminate and deport seventeen million Americans, mostly the leaders of religious, economic, and governmental groups? About the same percentage now had been liquidated in the Soviet Baltic countries and the same thing had happened thirty years before in the Caucasus, and to other nations in Asia.

He thought that nothing more tragic could happen to a nation than occupation by a brutal system which not only subjugates and exploits its population for the sake of the glory and achievements of the system, but even forces its victims to pretend happiness, smile, and call their oppressors liberators and beloved friends.

In his opinion the leadership of the Communist Party of the Soviet Union is of a criminal nature. They inflict cruel persecution on all, and especially on the smaller nations, but never admit this because they still recognize the difference between good and bad. They never admit the internal methods used in Soviet elections because they know elections are conducted in an indecent way. Anyone who knows that his behavior is wrong and tries to conceal rather than change it, is basically criminal.

This conversation fascinated me and impressed me very much. I couldn't help but pity him, even though he was a Communist, because he was a brilliant man gone astray, and there was no way in which he could alter his life.

We finished everything in Vilnius as soon as possible, and on February 20, Sunday, got airplane tickets and went to Moscow. At the Moscow airport we were met by the United Press correspondent, Mr. A. Koringold. He and his Russian driver took us to a new and beautiful American car. The short trip from the airport to Moscow in such luxury made a tremendous impression on me, and even more on my son. Apparently the inhabitants of Moscow are still not accustomed to American cars for when we stopped we were surrounded by curious people. Mr. Koringold brought us to one of the best hotels in Moscow, the Metropole. Without his help we would never have gotten a room there, much less two rooms with a bath and everything clean and beautiful. The price was only sixty rubles a day. The food in the cafeteria was good and in the evening there was an orchestra for dancing. The people were all well dressed. I could understand why foreigners visiting this beautiful city have no idea of Novostroika, Userda, or poor collective farms.

The next morning Mr. Koringold drove us to the Kremlin walls where we were photographed. There were a few other correspondents and a crowd gathered around us.

Johnny was not accustomed to such publicity and quietly told me, "Mama, I will run away."

Later we went to the American Consulate. Everyone was kind to us. No one can know how comfortable it is to talk to officials when you know they are telling the truth and trying to help you, not weaving a trap around you. We were processed there in less than a day.

The next morning we went to the Internal Ministry to get our foreign passes and at this point came another blow. A clerk explained that foreign passport regulations had been changed and we would have to go back to our former place of residence and request our passport there. I almost fainted. This was the moment I had been waiting for, the moment when someone would say, No one leaves the Soviet Union: now it had arrived.

We ran as quickly as possible back to the American Embassy and told them what had happened. They quieted my fears, saying that it was true such a new regulation was in effect, but they would try to find a way around it. The next day the American Consul told us that he had been advised that permission had been given to grant us the visas.

My daughter and husband were already in Copenhagen waiting for us.

That day I talked with John. It was the first time I had heard his voice in many years.

The next day we went again to the Internal Ministry, explaining that the passport had been promised. Again we were refused. We went back to the American Embassy and this time they set all of their machinery to work on our problem. In the afternoon they said that everything was ready.

18

Release and Reunion

THE NEXT MORNING, after a night of suspense, we went back to the Ministry and once more the clerk tried to push us out but I raised my voice. This embarrassed him and he went to his supervisor. It seemed that there had been some misunderstanding and we finally were issued the precious passports. This was on March 4, 1960.

We could leave that same afternoon on a Swedish airliner for Stockholm, or we could wait until the next morning and go on a Russian airplane directly to Copenhagen where John and Donna were waiting. The American officials had the same idea as I—get out of the country as quickly as possible. They advised me to go to Stockholm immediately.

As the airplane left the ground I felt that at last I was really free. We had our passports, the plane was Swedish, flying nonstop to Stockholm, and so we were out of Russian territory, forever.

A wave of happiness came over me, followed by a wave of rage and hatred because I realized what irreparable damage had been done to me and my family for no reason whatever. After all my planning and working and dreaming for so many years, I was suddenly afraid to meet John. I knew how much I had changed. Twenty years of suffering, fear, waiting, and physical hardship had changed me more than even I could realize, and what for? We were a plain ordinary industrious family who had harmed no one, who had only wanted the health and happiness of our children and a safe future for them.

For eight years I had worked like a horse, three years in deportation and five in prison, all to build Soviet power, and I had not been paid enough to stay alive. Without my husband's support I could not have survived to fulfill my "duty to socialism." Now I was afraid of the moment when he would see me—how would he accept me? How would he and Johnny see each other? I was not afraid to see my daughter, I only longed to know her.

The main events of my life passed through my mind. In vivid memory I saw fainting mothers beside the bodies of Lithuanian youths. I saw deportees, crying and shaking in the transports, I felt the constant hunger and fatigue of dirty Novostroika. Why should I be so fortunate compared with thousands of others? At least my life would have a happy ending. My boy had received his basic education and now before him was an unlimited future.

I thought of the thousands of Lithuanian deportees without permits to go home, living out their entire lives in terrible primitive poverty, powerless to give their children the education which might lift them out of these hopeless conditions, and I thought of all those who had come home without means, deprived of their property and status. All the oppressed Lithuanians, surrounded by lies, isolated from the rest of Europe—why should they suffer? Just because they belonged to a small nation which happened to be in the path of a giant?

Because we were occupied with these thoughts, our flight to Stockholm seemed very short. When the airplane doors opened we were surprised by hundreds of flash bulbs and many newspapermen. They surged forward, asking me about my experiences. Sometimes when I had dreamed of going to America I told myself that I would never tell in public what had happened to me. What good could it do? Hundreds of books had already been written about the indescribable sufferings in Russia, but they had had no effect. However, faced with the opportunity of explaining as best I could what it really was like, my resolution melted, and without hesitation I answered every question honestly and in plain language. I even talked on the radio.

Johnny and I spent that evening in a hotel in Stockholm. I talked to John again on the telephone and this time we were both rather shy because of the sudden publicity which surrounded us.

The next morning, March 5, we flew to Copenhagen. Near the ramp at the airport, I saw John and Donna. At first glance he looked much older and more tired than I had expected. We ran to each other, kissed, and wept together.

Again we were followed by newspapermen. Even the American Consul came to the airport to give Johnny his citizenship papers.

We stayed in Copenhagen two days because of bad flying weather. We spent the time together trying to escape newsmen and telling each other our stories. I was surprised to learn that they had paid over three thousand dollars in duties to the Soviet Union for the parcels sent to me over the years. I knew that John and Donna had fought for my release but I was the happiest woman in the world when I heard of the continuous struggle they had waged.

My daughter fascinated me. Who had given her such a strong love for her mother and the energy for such a struggle? How could she possibly remember me, my poor little Donna?

I was grateful to many important Americans who had spent so much time trying to get us out and united with our family. John told me that as long ago as 1941 the Director of the Superior Savings and Loan, Mr. DeRighter, had started steps in Washington to help me. Congressmen Young, Bender, Mrs. Bolton, Feighan (who was especially persistent), and Vanik had written numerous letters and pulled various strings. Mr. Jones, the secretary and legal counsel of Thompson Products, and his staff advised my husband and did whatever they could. The editor of the Cleveland *Press,* Mr. Louis Seltzer, had helped tremendously during the latter stages and had even financed John's and Donna's trip to Copenhagen. Mr. Al Ostrow of the Cleveland *Press* was the guardian and adviser of my husband and daughter through the last and most important part of the struggle and accompanied us on the trip back to Cleveland. His telephone calls from Copenhagen to Moscow officials had been a great help in obtaining our passports. Without the help of the Governor of Pennsylvania, Mr. Lawrence, who had arranged the meeting between Mr. Khrushchev and Donna, I would probably not be here now.

I regained my faith in humanity. If all these people had

been moved to help one family, somewhere there should be enough good-willed people to help a third of all humanity.

In New York we again were met by many newsmen, but we were anxious to go on to Cleveland as soon as possible. On the flight from New York to Cleveland the radio told us how many people were waiting for us at Hopkins Airport. Unfortunately, due to bad weather, we landed at Akron and came to our home by car at three in the morning. Nevertheless, even at that hour we found our entire house filled with people. My old friends from Cleveland had prepared an exciting welcome.

The old Lithuanian salt and bread greeted me. I must eat a little of each for good luck and success. There were so many who had fled from Lithuania in 1944 and whom I had not seen for sixteen years; they all wanted to know about friends and relatives, about my own experiences, about my trip home. Some newspapermen asked how I liked our new house, how I liked the colors that had been used, did I prefer electric or gas stoves (what a question for one who has had neither), and what refrigerator I preferred (any is better than none, I thought). These questions about simple household items impressed me. I had never had a refrigerator, not even when I lived in America before. I had never even seen one in Lithuania or Russia although I had heard that the Communist Party secretary in Pasvalys had a small one.

The next morning I looked at everything in the house. I opened the refrigerator, I turned on the stove, I looked out the window and saw two beautiful cars in our driveway similar to the one that had caused such a stir in Moscow. I looked at the fine furniture, the telephone, the TV. I remembered how we had lived twenty-five years ago in Cleveland, and could easily see how much progress this country had made. I don't think Americans fully realize it because the change has been gradual. Think how much an ordinary workingman can improve his life, compared with the world I had just left where all work is done under compulsion! There may be improvements in military factories, or big advances in rockets, or new levels of scientific discovery may be reached, but ordinary human beings, the workers, do not benefit.

I began to cry again, partly because of happiness and partly for the many I had left behind who have no hope of ever seeing better days. John came in while I was deep in memories and tears. He said, "Barbara, enough! You must leave your tears in Moscow."

I knew he was right. I must not live in the past but in the present and for the future. I must do what I can to let others know the truth, the real truth.